Close to my HEART *you'll always be,*
friends FOREVER, *you and me.*

PRESENTED TO:

_____

FROM:

_____

DATE:

_____

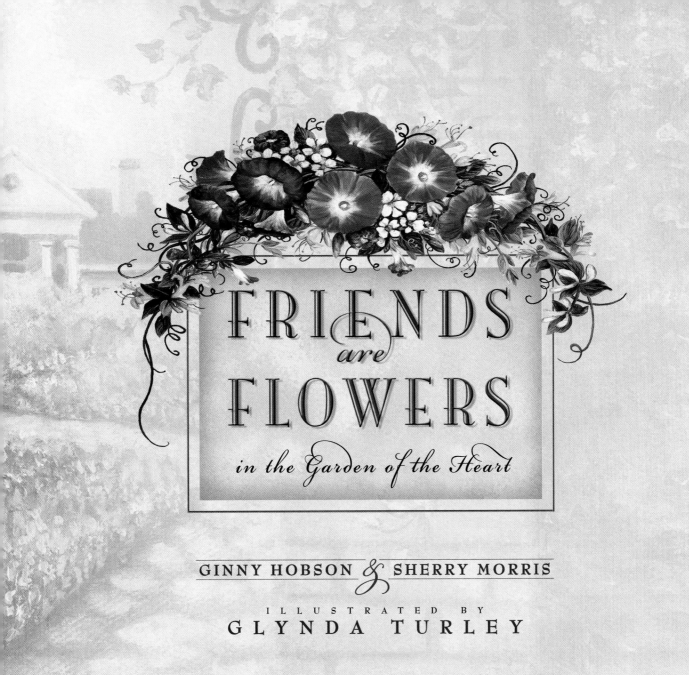

FRIENDS are FLOWERS

in the Garden of the Heart

GINNY HOBSON & SHERRY MORRIS

ILLUSTRATED BY

GLYNDA TURLEY

HONOR **HB** BOOKS

Tulsa, Oklahoma

THE CANVAS OF HER HEART

The beauty in artist Glynda Turley's life is painted
against a background of color from generations past.
As a nationally acclaimed artist, Glynda is loved for
her gift of creativity and artistic style that touches the
hearts of many. The canvas of her heart written here
also has many treasures for each of us to enjoy.

FRIENDS ARE FLOWERS IN THE GARDEN OF THE HEART

ISBN 1-56292-595-4

Copyright © 1999 by Ginny Hobson and Sherry Morris
THE CARPENTREE
P.O. Box 100
Tulsa, Oklahoma 74101

Published by HONOR BOOKS
P.O. Box 55388
Tulsa, Oklahoma 74155

Designed by: Lookout Design Group, Inc., Minneapolis, Minnesota

Scripture quotations marked NIV are taken from the *Holy Bible, New International Version* ®, NIV®.
Copyright © 1973, 1978, 1984 by International Bible Society. Used by permission of Zondervan
Publishing House. All rights reserved.

Scripture quotations marked NKJV are taken from *The New King James Version*. Copyright © 1979,
1980, 1982, 1994 Thomas Nelson, Inc. Used by permission.

Verses marked TLB are taken from *The Living Bible* © 1971. Used by permission of Tyndale House
Publishers, Inc., Wheaton, Illinois 60189. All rights reserved.

All works of art reproduced in this book are copyrighted and may not be copied or reproduced
without the artist's permission. For information regarding art prints featured in this book:
Glynda Turley, P.O. Box 112, Heber Springs, Arkansas 72543.

FRIENDS ARE EVER-BLOOMING
in the Garden of the Heart

Along the path of life, a garden gate stands open beckoning those who are willing to come inside. Its welcoming doors are carved from life's experiences and covered with remembrances. Come, find a place where the flowers of friendship grow.

As we walk through the garden, each friend is like a flower in life that is admired for its exquisite beauty and God-given design. Friends are treasured for their unique qualities and character traits that make them special to us. In the early days of friendship, the pansy friend borders our garden and brings to us the gift of being young at heart. As we grow older, we find that some friends are like the joyful sunflower who fills our lives with thoughtfulness and caring. Other friends are like lilacs of wisdom. The geranium friend blesses us when she stands up to the heat of life and is still a lovely fragrance. Pressed flower friends, though gone, are forever in the memories we often carry with us. Tulip friends come back to remind us of traditions shared as a family with our friends. Wildflower friends surprise us by the sheer fun they add to our days. And the rose, a true friend, is loved for the honesty she offers from her heart. Each friend adds lasting color and beautiful dimension, making the garden of the heart a place to celebrate.

Knowing something about the flowers in the garden helps us see our friends for who they are. Realizing that you can't make a wildflower a rose frees us from expectations. Just as flowers are uniquely different in the garden, we have the freedom to express our friendships differently to one another. Your wildflower friend may be a rose to someone else. You may be a sunflower to one friend and a tulip to the next. In the friendship garden, be yourself.

With the stories that follow, we hope to inspire you to recognize and understand the gifts and character qualities of all your friends. Whether they are sunflowers, tulips, or lilacs, our friends are cherished for the uniqueness and variety that makes them dear to us.

The love and care of friendship gardening is a lifelong joy. Some flowers are hardy and may not require much care. Others are quite fragile and need our frequent attention. Sometimes friendships wilt and need care to renew the relationship. Refreshing the soil and adding nutrients may help reestablish the roots of a friendship through an overdue letter, a spontaneous lunch date, or an encouraging phone call. Turning the soil in a garden adds fresh air for the roots to grow and so does a fun trip or trying a new idea together. (Scuba diving, anyone?) Sometimes we must pull the weeds of anger, hurt, or bitterness that may choke a friendship. To do this, we need the gentle garden gloves of forgiveness. Also, an occasional pruning adds growth to each flower. Loving honesty shared with a friend can sometimes hurt and even wound. But in time, the pruned flower may grow back stronger.

Let us go to the garden of friendship whenever we feel sad or lonely or disappointed. There we find renewal in the care of friends. Surrounded by a garden wall of acceptance, we can be restored and once again able to give to others. No matter what kind of day dawns or what joys or struggles life may bring, true friends are always there because *Friends Are Flowers in the Garden of the Heart.*

Ginny Hobson & Sherry Morris

CONTENTS

My Pansy Friend

GINNY HOBSON

The **PANSY** friend is a seedling
That blooms for the young at heart.
It's grown in the early days of life
Before "growing up" has to start.

Quite often a **PANSY'S** a sister,
Or maybe a school girlfriend.
But whoever she is, she is dear to our lives,
And our memories with her never end.

You are the **PANSY** in my garden,
A friend who has been there for me.
And you know that whatever life brings us,
Friends together, forever we'll be.

CHARACTER TRAIT
YOUNG AT HEART

Yesterday's a special memory until we meet again.
Time may pass, yet still we find we are the best of friends.

As children, we are beginning gardeners who feel an urgency to begin the season's planting. In our excitement to have a garden, seedling friends are quickly cultivated and watched to see if they will take root and grow. We just can't wait to find someone to be our friend. Hand in hand, friendships are made along with mud pies under the shade of a tree. Tea parties inspire long afternoons of camaraderie. "Ready or not, here I come" includes anyone who knows how to run and hide. Recess means that some friendships are formed, dissolved, and rediscovered in the span of about fifteen minutes. Just as the pansy borders the more formal flowers in the garden, childhood friendships teach us much about being a friend in preparation for our later friendships as women.

Some of us keep our seedling friends for a lifetime. Others are just kept in a journal of our hearts to remember fondly as we think back to a time gone by. Some of us are surprised to find that blossoms of friendship can be grown in the rich soil of our family. Sisters sometimes grow into the most beautiful flowers in our garden. What we learn as children from our seedling friends is transplanted into relationships that stand the test of time.

THE CARE OF A PANSY FRIEND ~ *Stay in touch!*

The distance and years between visits with a childhood or teenage friend can be long. In walking through the garden of your heart, remember these first flowers of friendship. Let the memories give you fresh motivation to write a long letter or pick up the phone to call a pansy friend. Sharing the laughter and remembering those days long past is a way to impart new life into your friendship. The early days of a friendship may once more take root and grow!

Friends Forever, You & Me

SHERRY MORRIS

Sherry, Sherry, friends need caring,
how does your garden grow?
With a fairy tale and memories shared
of little girls' hearts in a row.

Once upon a time there lived two little girls who didn't know each other until one day when Angie and I found ourselves in Mrs. Nanny's first grade class seated in a row of desks next to each other. The giggles and whispers from behind me got my attention even when my attention was supposed to be on the teacher. And that's how a friendship began.

In many ways, Angie and I were as different as night and day. Angie was outgoing, loved to act silly, and made friends easily. She had a hard time concentrating on dull and boring activities, like school. On the other hand, I was quiet, reserved and shy. My idea of a great day was to set the grading curve on a spelling test. Because of the differences in our personalities, Angie and I became close friends. I needed Angie to make me laugh. Angie needed me to take things like school, more seriously.

Angie and I grew up side by side, knowing each other's secrets from first grade on, and seeing the changes in each other that life and living bring. In second grade, it was obvious that Angie was resolutely in love with Elvis Presley. She even named her dog after him. Angie saw that I was madly infatuated with Donnie Thompson, a boy in my class. In fourth grade, I stood beside Angie in the school bathroom and patted her back while she cried and told me about the terrible fight her parents had the night before. In fifth grade, Angie was the one I called to tell about the conversations I overhead about my parents' divorce. When Angie and I played a piano duet together for a sixth grade recital, Angie's fingers froze and I played my part alone. Angie's mom and I had to convince her that "Yes, you will live and be able to go to school on Monday morning." Sixth grade was also the year that my dad, then single, asked Angie's mom for a date. In our minds, the possibility of becoming sisters was a logical and appealing evolution in our relationship. Unfortunately, our "shortsighted parents" didn't see it that way.

Like chalk drawings on a blackboard, school days are sketched into my mind forever. Angie and I took turns with the chalk and happily drew pictures in our hearts of slumber parties, dancing to 45 rpm records, holding "club" meetings on the playground, and many things both sacred and revered by two little girls who called themselves best friends.

In junior high, Angie and I wrote notes to pass back and forth between classes about who liked who and where we would go on Friday night, the mall or the movies. Carefully hidden from teacher's eyes, we shared the latest gossip and looked at life through the narrow condescending eyes of young teenagers. Always the notes were signed: "Friends 4-ever, you and me." In high school, the telephone replaced the notes, and topics of conversation grew more serious. In the '70s, I helped Angie to ponder some of the more important questions of life while cruising down the road in her Oldsmobile. Mostly though, Angie wanted to ponder who might be cruising down the road in the convertible next to us.

In college, Angie and I tried and gave up aerobics. Angie kept an extra set of keys to my dorm room because I set a school record for needing a replacement room key. Once, I found Angie crying on the front steps of the dorm after she broke up with her boyfriend. Together, we toilet-papered his car. Through thick and thin, good times and bad, Angie and I were there for each other.

In every once-upon-a-time story, there has to be a handsome prince. In this tale of Sherry and Angie, there were two handsome princes. One drove a black Chevy truck and the other a blue Gremlin. I was convinced that my bubbly best friend was about to kiss a frog who would turn out to be nothing more than a frog with a cowboy hat. Angie thought my choice in Prince Charming types came straight out of the land of long-haired hippiedom. Though we were bridesmaids in each other's weddings, both of us knew our lives were changing forever and our friendship might be entering the land-of-used-to-be.

Now living in different cities, one married to the cowboy hat and the other to the hippie, our circle of friends became separate. We were both busy starting our families and seemed to drift apart. For a while it seemed that forever friends only lived in the land of fairy tales, until one day, we found ourselves once again living in the same town. Now our conversations are shared when we are dropping off kids at school or over the occasional lunch we squeeze into our busy, grown-up schedules. The giggles and confidences we share are somehow familiar. It's just that now we talk about bosses instead of teachers, and children or husbands instead of parents.

Once-upon-a-time stories usually have a happily-ever-after ending. In the tale of Angie and me, happily ever after means that each of us knows in our hearts we really will be friends forever. Our friendship may not look the same as it once did on the chalkboard of long ago. But, we both know that being friends means going through the years with a tie of friendship that is held together by two hearts.

Besides, in a few years, the kids will be grown. Angie will probably convince me to take dancing lessons with her. I will remind Angie to go to her yearly mammogram. Chances are we will still be married to Steve (the Gremlin) and Charlie (the Chevy truck) which means that Angie and I will probably not spend Saturday nights playing cards together. Maybe someday we will all live in a retirement home together. I will distract the nurse so Angie can take Charlie's teeth and hide them in Steve's VCR. No matter how old they are, forever friends know how to have a good time!

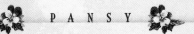
Growing Together Side By Side

JANE DEBORD

Opening their cheerful petals to the early light, pansies seem to dance and sway in the breezes of a new day. Jane's sister, Linda, was one of the earliest flowers to begin growing in the garden of her heart as she caught the first rays of friendly sunshine and nodded happily in the breezes of childhood.

What is that sound? Is there laughter in the garden? Do flowers laugh? They do when my sister is one of them! In my heart, she's always been like a pansy seedling, awake before spring to catch the first ray of sunlight. Growing alongside each other as sisters, just like seedlings from the same soil in the garden of life, wasn't something that we chose, but my sister Linda and I have always been thankful it happened that way because coming from that common ground gave us each other.

One of our earliest memories is captured in a faded photograph of the two of us—two little girls nestled together side by side on a wooden bench, the younger one tightly clutching a teddy bear. It is a perfect picture of our close relationship through the years—always huddled together, side by side. The teddy bear she holds in the photo was mine. Hers was ruined from being left outside for the rain and the pill bugs to destroy, and she cried so much that I gave her mine. We were born twenty-two months apart and have always thanked our parents for that, because we were close in age and also close in heart right from the beginning.

Simple pleasures of growing up together are preserved in the keepsake albums of our hearts because of the delight each moment brought—like going to sleep with the windows open and watching the sash on the curtain barely move in the quiet breeze that carried the scents of summer's fragrance and the sounds of the owl, the whip-poorwill, and the katydid. When the moon was full, its filtered light created a puppet show of leaves dancing on the wall. "Do you really believe there's a man on the moon?" she whispered. We would giggle and whisper, tickle and tell stories until we fell asleep.

My sister has always been able to find joy in the most ordinary events, or maybe just being together with her turns those ordinary events into times of joy. She is the most tenderhearted person I have ever known. She has rescued more frogs out of her swimming pool than I can count. As a teenager, she used to have a special one that waited for her on the porch every night when she would come in from a date. She would always say, "He's my Prince Charming, but I'm not going to kiss him to see if he will turn into a prince because I like him too much as a frog." Linda's love of nature still charms me.

My birthday is on Christmas Eve and often gets blended into the festivities of the holiday season. But my twelfth birthday was different. Each week we got an allowance of fifty cents, which we would usually spend together somewhere. But for several months, Linda would never spend any of her money. I didn't think much about it until later. On that Christmas Eve she called me into the kitchen. She placed a present on the table for me. When I opened it, I gasped at the beauty and uniqueness of the gift— an enameled jewelry box. Inside was a delicate ballerina dancing to the music of "Swan Lake," a tune we both loved. Tears filled my eyes as I realized how many allowances she had saved to give me this special gift.

A tapestry often depicts a picture of lovely flowers. When I think of the many special times Linda and I have shared as sisters, I see the threads of kinship crisscrossed and woven through our lives. All of my life, she has remained a friend, standing through the relentless elements of time, facing the chill winds of losing our parents, and braving the snows of life. If the tapestry is a picture of my friendship garden, there is a unique golden thread of friendship woven into it.

As I enter my own special garden of friendship, the scene that awaits me is always the same. Stretching to catch the first rays of sunshine in the morning's glad light is a beautiful pansy. She beckons all the other living things in my garden to join her and embrace the gift of friendship. A hum of conversation stirs among the other flowers who call out to me and say, "Who is that lovely pansy that calls us to rise and greet the new day?"

I smile and say with pride, "That's my sister."

No Bugs in Our Garden

BECKY DODD

Sue and I met in junior high. We didn't have the same friends or interests, so we never noticed each other until one summer, when we found we had something in common—the need for a friend.

Sue was pretty and popular with the boys. She was fun, friendly, and bubbly. But she had few female friends, and they were fickle. They bounced in and out of her life, riding on the wave of her popularity. Sooner or later the "jealousy bug" would bite her would-be friends. Sue's friend would date a boy who got caught looking Sue's way or a could-be boyfriend would ask Sue out. Then her would-be friends would be no more. On the other hand, I was incredibly shy and, in my eyes, not the least bit pretty. I never knew what to say, where to look, or where to put my hands when someone talked to me. The few persistent ones who helped me become more comfortable became my dear friends.

One summer Sue and I went to church camp. No one I knew was going, so I dreaded the week. Sue had come to camp with one of her friends, but the jealousy bug bit her friend the first day, so Sue was alone during free time. It isn't Sue's nature to dread anything. She was determined to have a good time, and she wasn't doing it alone. I was the loner in the cabin during our free time, and Sue noticed. She invited me to "goof off." For the first time in my life I was giggling and "girl talking" with one of the popular girls.

Our friendship flourished despite our differences. Sue's home didn't have the closeness mine did. She often came to my house, and my parents were like family to her. I'd never worn makeup before Sue taught me how. She gave me fashion tips and told me I was pretty. Like no one ever had before, Sue built up my self-esteem. I gave something to her, too: I wasn't jealous of her.

Sue will always be like a sister and my best friend. Though she lives miles away with her husband and daughter, she always manages to be a part of special things in my life, and I try to be a part of hers. She still knows how to make me feel good about myself when I'm down—a little lipstick and eye shadow and "girl talk"—and suddenly I feel special again. When she is upset that another "friend" has dropped out of sight, I remind her that we are best friends for life. No jealously bug can ever destroy our friendship.

My Tulip Friend

GINNY HOBSON

My FRIENDSHIP with you
Has grown over time.
Years of your family's fun
Are remembered with mine.

Our HEARTS shared the memories
Of friendship and laughter.
We've found that real friends
Are forever and after.

In my garden of friendship
The TULIPS stand strong,
For each year they come back
To where they belong.

So, THANK YOU for being here
Through the joy and the pain,
And I'll be here for you
In the sunshine and rain.

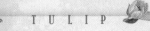

CHARACTER TRAIT
SHARING

Side by side or far apart, friends are always close at heart.

Side by side, tulips of the heart grow into beautiful flowers. Tulip friends often come along in the springtime of our lives as women. They are discovered when we find someone who shares a dream with us, or someone who is living in the same stage of life we are. The first blooms of a tulip friendship may grow as we spend time with a friend who also has children about the same age as our own.

Second generation tulips also grow in the garden of friendship. Learning to be friends is something children discover from watching "big girls" playing or talking together and sharing in each other's lives. Little hearts are often hand in hand beside us planting friendships of their own.

From birthday parties to vacations spent together, memories are shared between generations of tulip friends. Having tulip friends creates a unique sense of belonging that is almost like family. Tulip friends find that they are "all there for each other" in the good times and the bad. Even if miles separate their homes, their hearts are never apart. Connected by memories, tulip friendships bloom year after year.

Whether a first generation tulip or a tulip friend discovered in mother's friendship garden, these are friendships kept with the hope that a new generation will discover the joy of having and being a tulip friend.

THE CARE OF A TULIP FRIEND — *Just take time for them.*

Tulip friends need lots of room in the garden and years to grow. We may see them often or it may be just a Christmas card that keeps us in touch. Whether we see them often or rarely, remembering the times spent together and events shared connects us with our tulip friends. They can make our lives rich with a heritage of family tradition and friendship if we just take the time to be with them.

When Dreams Are Planted

MARTHA MEEKS

Knowing what a beautiful flower the tulip becomes when it begins to bloom in the spring is what makes us put it into the ground with a hopeful heart. Hidden beneath the surface, it lays waiting for the sunshine to warm the soil before it begins to grow. Some dreams are like the tulip. They are planted with expectancy and with the hope they will come into full flower at some time in our lives. When their dream was shared, Pam and Martha discovered how a friendship can grow.

I could hardly believe what I was hearing. A couple my husband and I knew from church wanted to adopt a child from East Asia. My family had the same dream planted in our hearts. Over the slow months that followed, Pam and I would grow to trust each other with our deepest thoughts and to cry with and encourage each other.

In the autumn of that year as the leaves blew over the windswept ground, we began to talk together about the children we wanted to complete our families. Just as springtime seems so far away from autumn's chill winds, our dream was months, maybe even years away. But during that time of waiting, our roots of friendship were forming and growing strong. It was the hope Pam and I shared that brought us together, but it was the care and concern we shared that made us friends.

It helped so much to have a friend who real-ly understood. Some people, even close friends, think that adoption is easy because there is no phys-ical burden to carry the child. Maybe that is why God knew Pam and I needed each other so much. Only Pam truly understood the heartache and stress of wanting and waiting for a child who was so far away. When a woman adopts a child, there are no doctor's appointments to schedule or ultrasounds to anticipate. Pam and I talked about our feelings of wanting something to fill the space and the time in our lives. But there was no heartbeat to hear or the kick of a little foot in the rib to fill the months while we waited for our babies. At times we were giddy with anticipation. But there were days when we just cried together, overwhelmed by the need to touch and hold the children we knew were "out there" waiting for us. I was so glad to have a friend who truly understood how I felt.

Several times a week, we called each other to check for any news. When I was down, Pam's encouraging words were welcome, because she really did understand. There were also days of joy. "I have pictures of her!" I said gleefully. Again, Pam rejoiced with me like no one else could. There were days of intense disappointment. "There's been another delay," I would say sadly. Pam knew that "another delay" felt like a lifetime.

Pam's adoption process started months before mine. How hard it must have been for her to hear that my adoption was picking up speed. I marveled at her strength. She focused all her energy on rejoicing with me and looking for ways she could help with the final preparations. All I could do was pray for Pam and her daughter—wherever she was.

On that wonderful day when our Amy came home, Pam was at the airport to meet us. There were many of our friends and family there to celebrate with us, but when I saw Pam's face in the crowd, I knew that she celebrated with me in a spe-cial way. Her eyes were full of happy tears and a smile beamed from across the room. In the second my eye caught hers, our hearts connected. I knew that she understood, like no one else could, the joy I was feeling. It was a grand day many months later when I stood at the airport and watched Pam and her husband return from China with their little girl. I, too, was there for her and blessed to be part of her joy.

Pam and I found that the ground from which our friendship grew was warmed by a dream shared. Now our two beautiful little girls with almond eyes play together while Pam and I talk about our dreams and plans for them. They are strapped side by side into car seats for a trip to the mall or the park. With full hearts, Pam and I now share the blessing of watching two amazing mira-cles growing to be buddies as well. When Amy and Taylor grow up, we will tell them the stories of how they became a part of our families. Part of that story is how their mothers shared a dream and became friends.

Through the Storm

JANE DEBORD

Little did we know as we made our way through National Guard checkpoints and scattered debris along the streets of Corpus Christi, Texas, that we were on our way to meet the couple who were to become our lifelong friends.

As the door of the apartment manager's office opened, a friendly young couple greeted us with smiles and good news that they had one vacant apartment left. Thus began our friendship with Danny and Ginny Hobson. My husband, Bert, and I could never have dreamed that being forced to move out of our "roofless" apartment would later result in the best times of our lives.

Seeds of friendship quickly sprouted as Ginny and I discovered that each of us was expecting our first baby a few months apart. Their daughter Jennifer was born in October, and our daughter Lara arrived the following March. Once a week we got together for playtime for both daughters and moms. Though our finances were meager, our favorite activity was to go out to lunch. All four of us "girls" would order from the children's menu. Our standard order was four "giraffes"—foot-long hot dogs with mustard and catsup.

As couples, Ginny and Danny and Bert and I developed a close friendship that would endure over time. One time, Danny wanted to go to an historical cave. The rest of us were not quite so enthusiastic. After several hints and suggestions toward his desired result, he said dejectedly, "Just forget it!" We all stopped talking and looked at each other and began laughing. From that moment on whenever someone wants to do something and someone else doesn't, we all laugh and say, "Just forget it!" It always puts the fun back into the day and makes us realize it's being together, not the plans, that are important.

When the girls were five years old, we excitedly called Ginny and Dan, who were now in Oklahoma, to tell them that we were expecting another baby in March—Michael. Ginny responded exuberantly that they were expecting another baby, too, in June—Daniel! Now we had made-to-order family friends with children the same age and sex, a perfect combination for vacations together. Our vacation budgets, however, were always limited. Thus began our famous "cheap thrills" travel agenda. We cut costs, often resulting in tight accommodations that made for laughter, fun, and growing experiences.

One year, on a winter ski trip, we booked reservations for a private home. Though the cost was within budget, based on the description we had great expectations of a luxurious home in the snow-capped mountains. After a flat tire and an all-night drive, we finally arrived at our home for a week—a two-bedroom mobile home with one bathroom for eight people. However, it was located in a "beautiful wooded setting." We knew we were in for the closest time ever together. Not to be deterred, we simply hung a bathroom schedule on the door, which worked well until the toilet backed up!

On one trip our boys got into a regular boy fight. Ginny and I were tempted to take our own child's side, but we decided that if we were going to keep our friendship strong, a no-fault policy had to be established. And so no matter what, we never took sides. Children and adults always worked it out—bathroom times and all. The lessons learned in tight accommodation spaces or in a cramped car taught us all how to give and take. Each of us grew to expect these little unforeseen occurrences to be turned around into something positive and even laughable. We would even joke, "Well, I wonder what's going to happen this time?"

On a trip to Corpus Christi, we stayed at a beach house, again with only one bathroom. By this time, we were all experienced. After a whirlwind trip to the Mexico border, five of us became ill with "tourista"—again not good with one bathroom! I can still visualize Ginny and I plopped on the bed and lamenting, "This is going be the trip that can't be salvaged—how can we possibly turn this into a good time?" Our children were the instrument of change. They had purchased string puppets in Mexico and, though all four were sick, they were determined not to let that stop them from having a fun time. The girls wrote a clever story and coerced their little brothers into participating in a puppet show that entertained us. And the "quick intermissions" (trips to the bathroom) with every scene also provided a good dose of laughter, which turned out to be just the needed medicine. That puppet script is stored in our trip memorabilia— now an heirloom.

As the flowers of our friendship have blossomed in the warmth of sunny seasons, its deep roots have also weathered the storms of winter: job losses, parents' deaths, and financial difficulties. Through the storms Ginny and I did not walk alone—God sent us each other to help in difficult days. We learned the power of prayer and trust in God.

Our daughters seem to be following in our footsteps. Last year, Ginny and Jennifer flew to meet Lara and me in Dallas for a mother-daughter weekend. We took pictures once again of the "four girls" only this time Lara and Jennifer were pregnant. Ginny and I became grandmothers together, as both of our girls had little boys two months apart.

This past May, when Bert and I were in Dallas celebrating our grandson's first birthday, the phone rang. As I overheard the conversation, I could tell that Lara was talking to Jennifer. I listened to non-stop laughter just as they had done as little girls so long ago. They were planning a get-together for both families so they could each meet the newest family members, when Lara suddenly began to exclaim: "Oh, you don't mean it. I can't believe it! Are you serious? I can't believe it's happening again—wait till I tell Mom." Lara yelled, "Jennifer's pregnant!" This completely dumfounded me as Lara had just announced her own pregnancy to us that same week. "Our due dates are one day apart!" Lara said, looking at me with a huge smile while she was still on the phone.

All I could say was, "I think I'll faint."

Sometimes I think back to that summer in 1970 when Hurricane Celia cut a path through Corpus Christi, and I remember the destruction—yes, but more than that, I remember the beautiful friendship that blossomed in its wake that might not have been if a storm had never come.

A friend is a seed

you sow with love

and reap with

thanksgiving.

A Legacy of Friendship

VIRGINIA BRADFIELD

As I awoke in the hospital after giving birth to a baby who had lived only five days, my emotions entwined with my physical and emotional pain. My baby girl was to be buried that afternoon. *Oh, no,* I thought with tears in my eyes, *I didn't get a bonnet for my baby.* I remembered my dear friend, Mavis, who was a pediatric nurse in the delivery room when my other two daughters were born. I knew she would help me. "Of course, she has to have a bonnet," Mavis said tenderly. She found one made of pure silk and tiny lace, and she had a nosegay of flowers made to place in my baby's hands. I will never forget the love she showed me that day. I was too sick and distraught to go to the funeral, so Mavis went for me and stood beside my family.

Mavis and I have known each other for more than forty years now. Our friendship began when we were each newlyweds. Since my nearest family was 700 miles away and Mavis was an only child, we became like sisters. Over the years, our families knit together as our lives crisscrossed with memories shared in fishing trips, picnics, and holidays. As our families grew up, we shared our children's graduations, weddings and, at last, our grandchildren. We agree—we should have had grandchildren first!

A few years ago, I was very sick. Mavis came to my hospital bedside, assisting my daughters as they gave me twenty-four hour care. While I was ill and near death, Mavis whispered to me, "Virginia, you just have to get well. Now, I won't have it any other way." She stroked my hand, and her tears told me something my heart knew—that we share a wonderful, precious friendship. We didn't want to go on without one another.

Mavis has been a part of every major event in my daughters' lives. We spend Christmas Eve at Mavis' home, and the Fourth of July is celebrated at my home with fried chicken, Mavis' famous chocolate cake, and plenty of fireworks. My daughters tell me they have learned how to be and have a true friend by watching Mavis and me. It is hard to even imagine what it would have been like to have never shared every crisis, every joy, and even all the "regular things" that Mavis and I have shared. A true friend is a treasure of the heart and someone no one should be without. We also hope they will teach this to our grandchildren—and the generation after—so Mavis and I can sit together and watch them all shoot fireworks in my backyard.

My Wildflower Friend

SHERRY MORRIS

Winsome & WHIMSICAL, wacky & wild,
A wildflower friend is a grown-up child.
She knows how to laugh—how to have a good time.
She sees everyday as an adventure to find.

Spontaneous and CARING, joyfully daring;
At a party, she'll want to know what you're wearing.
A wildflower friend has a tale, maybe two—
A joke or fun story that she'll share with you!

Playful and LOVING, vibrant, not pale;
Don't bother this friend with the time or the mail.
She's the one who you call when you're feeling quite sad;
Soon you'll be thinking, "Hey, life's not so bad!"

Friendly and BREEZY, all around pleasing;
Quite warm and sunny throughout every season.
A wildflower friend is a friend I adore,
You, my dear friend, are these things and more!

CHARACTER TRAIT
JOYFULNESS

Time together is time well spent.
Time with a friend is heaven sent.

Along the path of life, some flowers just appear on the landscape whose purpose seems to be to add a splash of color and whimsy to our lives. Blowing through their merry hearts are playful winds. Unexpectedly, they wave to us and invite us to stop and spend some time having fun. The wildflower friend always has a joke and several stories to tell about her life, even if we just saw her yesterday. She knows how to have fun. She is quick with ideas of what to do with the day. Seldom do you find a wildflower friend alone, at least not for long. Often, we find wildflower friends through the activities we share. A spontaneous flower, she may pop up anywhere. She's the friend who wants to go get ice cream without the kids, knows a practical joke you should play on your husband, or has a hare-brained adventure she's sure you'll just love.

In the company of a wildflower, joy, playfulness, camaraderie, and just plain fun find their way into an ordinary day. Sometimes the wildflower adds only a fleeting bit of color for a few years to our lives before she moves on to some other new venture or activity. Other wildflowers are a hardy lot and remain along the roadside to decorate our days for many years to come. Whatever the case, joy is a gift from her life she is always happy to share!

THE CARE OF A WILDFLOWER FRIEND — *Give them freedom to grow.*

Wildflower friends need lots of freedom. They meander, pop up, and grow anywhere! Don't try to restrict a wildflower with rules of friendship. They usually don't follow any. They are not the type of person who will invite you to "show me your deepest feelings." The wildflower friend is the "let's go and try this" variety of friend. Usually what they want to do is some never-tried adventure. Let them be free—we can't get upset if they don't call when they should or show up on time. They are just "wild," and that is, after all, what we love most about them!

Landing Feet First

SHERRY MORRIS

Just as Ethyl had a friend named Lucy, I have my friend Trish. She doesn't have Lucy's signature red hair, but she does have an unfailing nose for mischief. She's not married to a Cuban Ricky, but her husband rolls his eyes and mutters unintelligibly whenever she comes home telling of her latest encounter with near disaster. Wherever Trish goes, some kind of misadventure follows that leaves everybody laughing or that gets somebody—like me—in trouble. The amazing thing is that Trish is always genuinely shocked when she doesn't look before she leaps and things don't always turn out like she planned. But somehow she always manages to land feet first.

Having a friend like Trish is a joy. Just watching her life is very entertaining. But more than that, Trish is a tender and caring person. She listens to my problems when I am down and I can always count on her to make me laugh. Many people know that Trish's precarious sense of humor has a way of leaving people tottering on the edge of not knowing whether to laugh or just shake their heads in disbelief.

When Trish and I start out working on a project together, I have learned to expect the unexpected. For example, we decided to have a Nickelodeon party for the kids at our church. We filled two 50-gallon garbage cans with slime made from flour, green food coloring, and water, prepared 200 water balloons for our Double Dare Bible Game Show, and fixed 10 cream pies for our version of the infamous pie pod. While I stood outside giving Trish some last minute instructions for the game show, my impulsive friend decided that I should experience the first pie in the eye—in spite of the fact I still had a committee meeting to go to before I could go home and change.

If it had been anyone but Trish who pie-eyed me, I would have been furious. Instead I just went to the meeting. "I was preparing for a party with Trish," was all the explanation needed as to why my hair was sticky and plastered to my head in places.

According to our original plan, we were going to have a controlled "slime-filled" event. Before the afternoon was over, Trish had instigated a slime free-for-all. Slime flew everywhere—on the kids, on the sidewalks, on the equipment, and on parents who happened to be standing by. Children had to be hosed off before going home. Some of our more stoic parents looked at us as if we were bereft of our senses. The only sense I had left at the moment was the sense to go find a lot of towels. I also sensed I was going to have to face

a ringing phone and irate parents on Monday morning. "Oh well," said my friend with a typical Trish philosophical shrug, "No one got hurt and we had a great time!" She was right about that— *all* the kids, including Trish, had a great time. Monday came and went with none of my imagined repercussions for her folly. Somehow, once again Trish fell headlong into another adventure and landed feet first.

My friend came walking into church not long ago with a multi-colored cast on her leg (coordinating toe nail polish to match). She claimed she had fallen down some stairs, but just knowing Trish, I knew that couldn't be the whole story. Said an eyewitness, "We were walking along inside a building when Trish spotted a long staircase with a wide banister. Now just why seeing a staircase with a banister brought out the inner child in this normally responsible mother of two, I don't know." It seems that the next thing she saw was Trish flying down the banister with the winds of impulsiveness blowing through her hair. It was a ride that went well until the end. Once again Trish landed feet first. But this time she broke her foot.

I realized not long after that incident just what it is I find so appealing about Trish: her impish inner child invites me outside my "stick to the rules" self to play sometimes. Somehow when that happens I am able to forget what a busy mother I am with multiple responsibilities both at work and at home. When Trish calls to tell me something about her wild and crazy day, I feel a vicarious sense of participation in something ridiculous and fun. When I call to remind her of some responsibility she needs to remember, she always finds a way to make me laugh and not take anything quite so seriously.

There will probably be other adventures like the Nickelodeon party in my future experiences with Trish. I may have a wild ride down the banister of friendship with the winds of misadventure blowing through my hair, never sure whether to laugh or scold. But there is one thing I have learned from my wildflower friend; it doesn't really matter what happens at the end of the adventure, it's all the fun we have on the way.

The Wildflower That Flourished

LORENE HOPKINS

A wildflower, "unexpected and spontaneous," certainly describes my friendship with Glennis. A bubbly, happy, fun person, she often calls for a quick lunch date or a get-together time in unexpected places. A builder's wife, she has a great knack for decorating the homes her husband builds, and her ideas are creative and different. She was also a teacher and could recognize the creative spark in a student when others thought of them as "departing from the norm." She always inspired the less motivated students.

Glennis seems to know when to add her special color to my days. This past year, I was critically ill and just home from a long stay in the hospital. I was sitting alone in my bed recuperating from surgery trying to interest myself in books and TV shows, when Glennis arrived with two gourmet lunch boxes, a centerpiece, table goods with eating utensils of every description, and a stack of beautiful magazines for me to enjoy. We had a "party for two" as we celebrated my recovery. What joy she brought to me that day!

Sometimes Glennis makes me think of the wild sweet pea that continues to bloom for each new generation. When I planned a fortieth birthday party for my son, it was Glennis who provided the laughs and memories of the day. She knew that our son was involved with a top-of-the-line clothing store. He was an expert at combining suits, shirts, ties, and accessories for men, so she searched high and low in thrift stores until she found "just the right" shirt and tie. She had them cleaned, pressed, and beautifully wrapped in an exquisite gift box. It took a few minutes for everyone to realize the gift was a shocking out-of-date pattern, a terrible combination of color, and made of the worst materials imaginable. She presented it to our son with a loving smile. At first stunned, but determined not to show her how awful it looked, our son said, "Oh! Now there's a tie and shirt for you!" Glennis exploded in laughter.

When I think of Glennis, I think of the tenacious trumpet vine that roots and spreads along the fencerow proclaiming its triumph over nature with the brightest of orange flowers. We went through a very deep personal valley of despair at one time in our friendship, but Glennis came springing back slowly like the wildflowers along the roadside. The seeds of hope sustained her and the roots of her determination to make things work for her family prevailed. Even wildflowers can have deep roots.

Choosing Joy

GINNY HOBSON

About twelve years ago a new family moved into our "neck of the woods" and immediately I loved being around this engaging, fun, adventurous girl. She offered me a slice of carefree days that were foreign to my seriously scheduled, overly organized, "under the gun" life.

Kathy always has a way of making an ordinary day extraordinary. A phone call from Kathy is an invitation to come out and greet the day, and often at 6 a.m. when I am still trying to focus. Sometimes she would frustrate me because she took things so lightly, but I always wanted to do things with her because she brought such joy and spontaneity to my life.

Her first winter in our neighborhood, Kathy noticed that there was mistletoe hanging from a tree branch. I had walked by that tree for five years and never noticed it, but she did. So she said, "Let's go get some!" The next thing I knew my friend was high on a tree branch while I balanced a ten-foot ladder. Then I heard the branch snap and crash. I took her, limping, to the hospital where the nurse gave me the instructions for the crutches, medications, ice, and ace wraps. When I drove up to her house, her husband, Bill, greeted us with an icy stare. I could tell that there had been other perilous events he had witnessed with similar results. I was pretty sure Kathy didn't get a kiss under the mistletoe that night.

When spring came, she asked me, "Want to plant a garden?" I agreed, thinking this would be a great teaching time for my five-year-old and me. But forty-two tomato plants, broccoli, cabbage, cucumbers, squash, and every bug known to mankind later, I was a hay-chewing farmer—canning, freezing and frying. When Kathy planted a garden, it was for the whole hundred-acre woods with food for every man, woman, child, rabbit, squirrel, fox, raccoon, deer, and bug—we fed them all for miles around! "Come on, Gin," she'd say, "this will be fun," as we hoed, toiled, weeded and picked. Achy, sore, and covered with chiggers, I wasn't quite convinced. But she made it sound so great!

One day she bought a new shotgun. "Let's go hunt snakes," Kathy said.

My experience with snakes was to look-see-run. Now she wanted to go find-see-shoot. And we did. The poor four-foot green garden snake (mistook in a fit of panic for a brown copperhead) never had a chance against a double barrel shot gun pointed at his head.

One Christmas, Kathy encouraged me to buy horses for our boys. *Okay*, I thought. Never mind that the boys are too young to take care of them and that she and I will end up feeding, watering, brushing, and otherwise caring for the animals. What had she gotten me into now? It was almost a year after we bought them when our sons became physically big enough to take over. But I have to

admit we had a lot of fun during those months playing cowgirls. She tried to teach me the proper way to cinch a saddle. Unfortunately, the horse knew her plan and blew out his stomach so that when I cinched and tried to climb on, both the saddle and I went from seeing the world from the top of the horse to viewing things from under the horse's belly. And Kathy would just laugh and encourage "Annie Oakley" to ride again.

One day on one of our "dawn patrol" excursions, we rode and talked about being wives and mothers. Kathy could talk about serious things as long as there was a punch line in the conversation somewhere. I crested a hill and watched a whole flock of Canadian geese fly into the air just a few feet from where we were. "Kathy," I exclaimed with excitement, "Did you see it? Wasn't it beautiful? I've never seen anything like this before. I am so glad we came!"

Kathy was nowhere to be seen. I turned my horse around. "Gin," I heard a faint voice say from a clump of bushes, "I'm over here." My friend was lying flat on her back with a scrunched look on her face. I gasped and half-laughed at the sight, yet I knew being thrown from a horse wasn't so funny. "I'm okay," she said, "I'm just stiff."

Six months later, after trying therapy and pain pills to no avail, my friend had spinal neck surgery to correct the damage from the fall. For the first time she had to slow down. I had never seen such a pained look on her face, and it brought sadness to my heart. Undaunted, she came through, but there was to be no more horseback riding.

Soon the winds of change would dampen her spirit even further. Her husband, Bill, became ill with cancer. He was the sole provider of their family's income and self-employed. Kathy knew she needed to look for work. Suddenly, they were in a swirl of confusion and fear. Prayers were lifted night and day. My fun friend, with the laughter in her heart and always a song for everyone was filled with worry. After days of not eating, she collapsed and was hospitalized. When I visited her, she wasn't the same person I had known. My happy-go-lucky friend was nowhere to be found. And it was then I knew she needed me and her other friends to comfort and love her, just as she had given joy and fun to us. It took some time, but Kathy slowly recovered her frolicsome spirit. This time, though, there was a deeper and more mature quality to her joy.

Kathy shared with me about the changes in her heart. Her husband, thankfully, is much better. Instead of climbing trees and riding horses to find joy, Kathy says that now she begins each day under the mantle of prayer and waits expectantly for the gift of joy that God gives her life. Joy is more than just being playful and having fun; it comes from a heart that is at peace in knowing God will take care of each day. Some days, joy is a choice. So now Kathy wears a pin that says "choose joy" to remind her of the choice she makes every morning.

She still has a sense of fun about her. She still has a joke or a story to tell or a song to sing for all her friends. And when I think of my friend Kathy, I have to smile. For in spite of all life has brought her, she still chooses joy every day and then gives it gladly to others.

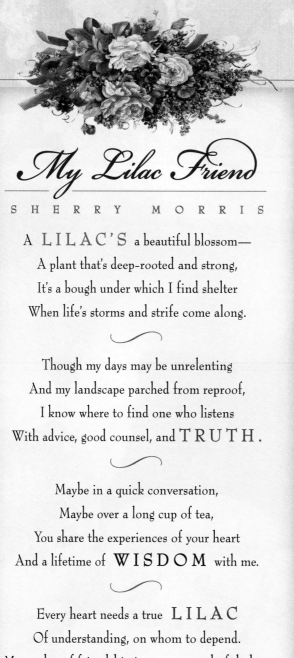

My Lilac Friend

SHERRY MORRIS

A LILAC'S a beautiful blossom—
A plant that's deep-rooted and strong,
It's a bough under which I find shelter
When life's storms and strife come along.

Though my days may be unrelenting
And my landscape parched from reproof,
I know where to find one who listens
With advice, good counsel, and TRUTH.

Maybe in a quick conversation,
Maybe over a long cup of tea,
You share the experiences of your heart
And a lifetime of WISDOM with me.

Every heart needs a true LILAC
Of understanding, on whom to depend.
My garden of friendship is a more wonderful place
With you in my life, my friend.

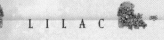

CHARACTER TRAIT

WISDOM

A friend is someone who listens with her heart.

A friend who is a lilac in the garden of the heart is the friend who mentors us. Her roots are firmly set in the soil of years. Often this friend has weathered the storms of life, allowing herself to be pruned and shaped by winds of living and years of experience. Because of her resiliency, she has grown full of wisdom and strong in character. These friends often offer us shade under branches of encouragement. Sometimes they shelter us from the heat of discouragement or a torrent of tears. When a crisis or difficult time comes, they offer a word of wisdom, a note of love, or a lifting hug. The lilac friend's welcome shade adds refreshment and renewal to our lives. Often older and stronger because of their years, lilac friends offer "cuttings" from the branches of their experiences. They may give us the very insight we need to see a problem in a whole new light. We may take a cutting from their branches of forgiveness or gratitude. A cutting may be a lesson shared that gives us a different perspective and allows us to plant this branch into the garden of our own experiences. From these firm roots, we can then share "life lessons" with others. A cutting from this beautiful and established tree adds fragrance and wisdom that may change us forever.

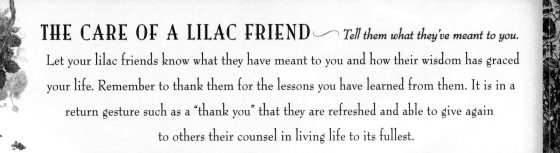

THE CARE OF A LILAC FRIEND — *Tell them what they've meant to you.*

Let your lilac friends know what they have meant to you and how their wisdom has graced your life. Remember to thank them for the lessons you have learned from them. It is in a return gesture such as a "thank you" that they are refreshed and able to give again to others their counsel in living life to its fullest.

A Lilac in My Path

JENNIFER HOBSON LAMB

I first met Jadine when I was a young teenager. She is ten years older than I am, and almost immediately I wanted to be like her. The first thing we had in common was our love of cheerleading. She had cheered for years in high school and college, and I wanted to be a cheerleader so bad I could taste it. So, she volunteered to be my personal coach for tryouts. For three years of tryouts she would practice with me everyday after school—on everything from toe-touches to eight-count dance routines. The second year, Jadine became a mom, and little Kristen watched as we practiced together. I jumped so much in her yard, her husband never could get the grass to grow in "my space" again!

Although my first attempt at tryouts was unsuccessful, Jadine still showed her confidence in me and helped me to look beyond my fears and self-imposed limitations. She just said, "Jennifer, God knows our heart's desires. I know you can keep praying for and working toward this goal." Her words still echo in my life today. She always sees me as a person packed with potential, and my self-esteem never has a chance to dwindle around Jadine.

Jadine was so giving to me during high school and college—those years of new experiences and the uncertainty that comes with them—she always had time for me. Whether it was an unannounced visit after school, or a phone call at 2 a.m., she could help me sort out my perplexed feelings—and help me clear up the muddy waters. From relationships with guys to prioritizing activities, she had an open ear or a shoulder to cry on. Her advice was always given in a loving, yet challenging manner. She noted the benefits of choosing a biblical path without compromise.

Like a lilac grows full and provides needed shade in my path, Jadine offers me a place to stop and rest and listen to my heart so that I can face whatever may lie ahead. Her support, concern, and love for me mirrors that of a sister, mother, and friend combined. From physical training to spiritual discernment, or even parenting techniques, she has shown me so much. I've learned from her never to give up on my goals and to keep them in line with God's will. I've also learned from Jadine's willingness to take time from her busy day to spend with me that people—not things or work or activities—are the most important.

When I was preparing to get married and choosing my bridesmaids, it was easy to pick my closest friends. But when the choice for a Maid of Honor came up, my mom and I looked at each other and both said, "Jadine." My mom has always been grateful that Jadine was my mentor and helped keep me on the right path.

And so it's to Jadine that I still go when I'm feeling unsure of how to handle what's ahead. I remember a time not long ago when I rang the doorbell at her house once again. She came to the door, embraced me and my pregnant tummy with lots of love, and again showered me with understanding. Now the mother of three, Jadine could give me the perspective I needed to help me sort out all my doubts, questions, and fears about becoming a mom. Settling comfortably into a familiar chair in her family room, I poured out my heart while she poured us some tea. "I'm so excited for this baby to get here, but sometimes I can't help but worry what things will be like when the time comes," I said with all the uncertainty I had felt for weeks. "I wonder how our lives will change. And I know David wonders, too."

Jadine asked me questions about our plans and situation. Amazingly once again, she offered both empathy and solutions to help me be sure I did the right things—physically, emotionally, and spiritually, to prepare for the arrival of my baby. My fears began to melt with her heartfelt guidance.

This God-given friend truly helped me mature through my growing-up years. She has offered me a sincere gift of friendship. She has given me "roots" I might never have had. The path to Jadine's house is never long. I feel she continues to be a mentor and a friend to me in more ways than she will ever know. I pray that someday I, too, will be a lilac in the life of a friend.

My Before-and-After Friend

DIANE VILLINES

I divide my life into two periods:
"Before Virginia" and "After Virginia."
"After Virginia" began in 1972
when we met. Without knowing
she was doing so, she fine-tuned my
thinking and changed my life completely.

When we first met, I was thirty years old and single. Virginia was a bride of nine months with a large, blended family. We shared a small office space, and I was immersed in her life as I heard her soft, affectionate telephone conversations with her husband, saw her gentleness with the five teenagers she nurtured into loving one another as though they were blood kin. I watched her manage her money with the greatest dignity and common sense, and I loved her hospitality in the warmth of the house she made into the sweetest home.

One thing I learned from watching her life from the other side of our office was that I wanted a marriage like Virginia's. I longed and prayed for partnership, contentment, honesty, friendship, integrity, love and devotion. By the grace of God, the perfect man came into my life. Virginia's sturdy spirit and deep love of family life had readied me to recognize him. Before Virginia, I didn't know what I wanted or thought about marriage. After Virginia, I knew without a doubt how I wanted to live my life.

My twenties had gone by without my thinking much about children. I saw no children in my future. Then, Virginia told me about a child she had lost many years before, "You know you expect to lose your husband, but you never expect to lose a child. It's the hardest thing I've ever had to do." I couldn't get the conversation out of my mind. I kept thinking that if losing a child is the most traumatic thing a woman can ever experience, then what will I miss if I never have a child? But when I married in my thirties, I was fortunate enough to have a child. I found being a mother to be the finest and dearest blessing ever presented to me.

Over the years, Virginia's blended family ballooned into more than a dozen grandchildren. She is "Nana" and her patience with kids and grandkids alike is legendary, as is her not-so-subtle, downright persistent nudges. She is a woman not to be put off when the well-being of her family is at issue. And, now that I'm a "Nana" myself, I love hearing my granddaughters Chloe and Katy calling, "Nana, come and read," and "Nana, I love you." Without Virginia, I would have never been a "Nana."

Virginia brought other friendships into ours that we've both treasured. Together, we lost several of these friends and from these losses we have made a promise to each other. No matter how ill we become, we won't keep the other from being a part of that time in our life, and our closeness will continue even in the anguish of pain or the sadness of death, just as we have cherished our closeness during the very best times of our lives.

My friend listens and listens, she supports, and she encourages. Our politics are worlds apart; we agree on nothing political, yet we do not care. Virginia—the Sicilian lady with her sweater jauntily tied around her neck, her olive skin smooth and fresh, her simple jewelry that's always just the right touch—has the heart of the most loyal and loving friend.

Borrowing Mother

S U E   R H O D E S   D O D D

When Mom and Dad moved 700 miles from their lifelong friends, the busyness of their retirement years helped deter their feelings of loneliness. For decades they had helped the New Orleans community—Dad as a Christian businessman and Mom as a homemaker who led a ladies' prayer group for more than twenty-five years.

They had opened their home to countless people who were hurting and seeking "something more" in their lives. Marriages were saved, alcoholics and drug addicts found their way to sobriety, and families found renewed—and lasting—harmony and faith. People facing disasters like hurricanes and floods or who were immigrants seeking safety and freedom in this country found immediate help and long-term hope from my parents.

It's no wonder that their "retirement" years were less than relaxing. They bought land on a peaceful lake in the Arkansas Ozarks and welcomed people needing a getaway. Guest cottages fittingly named Faith and Peace housed families, missionaries, singles retreats, students, and hundreds of people who came to pray, read, relax, and be renewed.

Yet with time, Mom and Dad had to leave that ministry, too, and take a real retirement in Tulsa, Oklahoma. Age and illness prevented them from continuing in such demanding roles. Dad's health took a downturn, and Mom found herself faced with his long-term healthcare and an unbearable loneliness. She was losing her life partner one day at a time.

Mom wondered, *Could God ever use me again to help people?* After a lifetime of touching thousands of lives and seeing the often-dramatic results of prayer, hope, and love, my mother found her own health was diminishing. She was losing her sight, and she felt isolated by her loss of independence. The years ahead looked long and burdensome—and lonely. *The days of ministry are over*, she thought. But God had a different idea.

One of my good friends had been single for more than a decade. In recent years, Judy lost both parents, and her siblings lived across the country. Though a delightful friend to many, Judy was childless and often felt the pangs of loneliness herself. She decided she needed a mentor, and my mother came to mind. My parents have long thought of Judy as one of their "adopted daughters," and the mutual admiration between my mother and Judy was already in place. Judy was unaware of Mom's discouragement, and Mom did not know Judy wanted a mentor. Judy called Mom, and suddenly my own phone line was jammed with both of them calling me to share their happy news. "I don't know if I can really help her," Mom said, feeling an odd mingling of wonder and doubt, "but I'm willing to give it a try."

It was a match made in heaven. Months later, I still can't find out which one of them enjoys this mentoring relationship the most.

I wondered if I would feel jealous of their growing relationship, but how can I begrudge either of them something that means so much to them both? Judy borrows my mother, and Mom has found yet another daughter. They go to dinner together. They talk for hours. They pray together. They laugh, they cry, they visit. Mom delights in hearing every detail of Judy's life, and Judy delights in the telling.

Fifteen years ago, my mother bid her prayer group friends goodbye. "We'll miss you, Sarah," many of them said. "It just won't be the same without you." And when she and Dad finally retired, she thought she said a last farewell to her years of serving others.

But my mother touches more lives than she realizes—just by being herself. A dental reception-ist tells me that Mom's sweet smile and delightful southern accent always brighten her day. A house-keeper says just being around my mother is a high-light of her week. A nurse watching my mother's tenderness toward Dad wipes away a tear and tells me how precious they are together. A secretary says she hopes she can be like my mother some day. A grumpy cashier watches with wonder at Mom's ability to "see" past her handicap. And Cheryl, Frances, Pat, MaryBelle, Lesa, Ann, and Emily adore her sweet spirit, her quiet wisdom, and her giving heart.

Mom's ability to help others continues—beyond what she could ever have imagined. For decades, the lilac fragrance of her life has been a blessing to all who know her. And in the December of her years, the lovely fragrance of Sarah has not faded. I have let countless women borrow my mother over the years. With wonder and more than a little healthy pride, I get to watch them help one another in ways I could not. How great is my joy!

My Geranium Friend

GINNY HOBSON

I've watched you face life's challenges,
And admired how you stood
Against the storms and winds of change
And wondered how you could.

It seems this inner strength you have
Is a stranger to my heart.
You draw from it then go once more
To face what life imparts.

I've admired your deep courage;
Your faith must be the key.
But through it all, no matter what,
You've been a friend to me.

You have been one of my heroes,
A hand you'll always lend.
And I've been blessed to know you
And have you as my friend.

CHARACTER TRAIT
ENDURANCE

"Love. . . hopes all things, endures all things. Love never fails.
I CORINTHIANS 13:7-8 NKJV

Friends who are like geraniums in the garden of the heart are those who have endured extreme circumstances in their lives. Like a flower grown from seed must sometimes overcome poor soil, not enough moisture, and any number of unfavorable growing conditions, some of our friends find themselves coping with events in life that seem insurmountable. Yet the geranium not only continues to grow, she grows stronger through the years. Many of us are blessed to have a geranium friend. We know that she is an inspiration to us because of her fortitude and steadfast heart. We see her spirit rise up and overcome the obstacles or difficulties faced, often with a smile still on her face. The geranium friend is a flower who knows that peace is found deep within a life well-rooted in faith. From this friend, we gather lessons about faith, hope, and love.

THE CARE OF A GERANIUM FRIEND ~ *Just "be there" for her.*

Geranium friends need to know you are there. They are not always the friends who seek you out as often as you would like. To be a friend to this friend who has gone through so much, you may need to be the one who calls or visits. Remember, it is this friend who can teach you much about how to go on whenever you encounter life's difficulties. It is just "being there" that counts with a friend who has taken the heat of life and pressed on.

To Lift My Head

JULIA MOORE

My insides felt like a black cauldron. *How could this be happening?* I asked myself over and over. *I had raised my children right, hadn't I?* I thought we had been such a model Christian family. Yet my oldest son, who had just graduated cum laude from college with his future awaiting him, had just called to tell his father and me that his girlfriend of only a short time was pregnant. He let us know that he had stopped a convenient abortion and had chosen to stay with her, raise the baby, and "maybe someday" get married.

"God," I cried out in my pain, "I remember turning this son over to You completely, because he has always been my challenging one. What went wrong?" Though I was proud of him for choosing to raise the child, I was so angry that he had disrupted his future with an act of selfishness. He and his girlfriend had not been more than acquaintances. She was only eighteen, and they were not even sure they wanted to get married. The situation was not at all what I had desired for my son. "God," I said sadly, "I gave him to You to grow him up and now look at this mess!"

Bearing our pain alone, my husband and I had no perspective, only terrible confusion. We were going about our daily plans and schedules in a state of numbness. We told no one of our grief. We left the next week for a three-day trip with some very dear friends. They have a beautiful family with a married daughter and two sons. While driving, I found myself sharing all of this with my friend Jena. My brokenheartedness and weakness were exposed as she listened.

Then the most amazing thing happened. Jena held my hand and said, "Julia, this is my story, too." It was as though I had been hit with a bolt of lightening.

"Your story?" I questioned. Jena told me that she, too, at age eighteen, had become pregnant after "the first time" with her boyfriend. It was suggested to her that she have an abortion as well. Both of their families were devastated. Jena had to quit college. Her boyfriend joined the Navy and moved 500 miles away. But Jena and her boyfriend loved each other. After the initial shock, their families gave them their blessing and they were married. Miles away from home and close to being financially destitute, the young couple awaited the arrival of the baby. Jena shared, "Those early days in our marriage were a time in our lives when we first began learning to rely on God. We struggled for years to raise our daughter, pay our bills, and finish college."

As she talked, I thought, *Look where they are today. The little girl they had so young is now a beautiful woman who just graduated from college. Their family has been a light to so many.*

As Jena told her own painful story and I saw how God worked through her impossible circumstances, I began to feel a soft light of possibilities come into my darkness. Jena helped me to see that, as a Christian, my only option was to love and accept. There was no other path to take if I believed in His mercy and grace. Above all else, she reminded me that God and His plan were greater than the apparent circumstances. God is a God of hope—a God who works in impossible situations.

That day my friend commissioned me into the mission field, to love beyond my human ability. As I relied on God to help me be open to His plan for my son, I began to see the possibility of bringing one of His truly lost ones into the saving grace of God. As Jena began to talk in terms of this pregnancy presenting me with my first grandchild, something awakened in me. The pain of it all and the death of my dreams had prevented me from personalizing this little life. I was going to be a grandmother!

The book I had written for my children read that they would date, fall in love, marry, establish careers, and then have babies. God showed me I had to begin a new book with empty pages and allow Him to write His possibilities and His plans. My head, along with my spirits, began to lift ever so slightly.

On a daily basis during the following months, Jena helped me as I went through times of "putting to death" my desires for my son. She helped me as we planned a wedding, watched sadly when my son's wife left him, and stood by me when my son went through a divorce. Today, my son is the single parent of an adorable little girl. He has a job with an excellent future, and a family who loves him, and his precious little girl, deeply. Looking back, I am in awe that God sent Jena to remind me of His unconditional love and to lift my head.

A Geranium Who Would Not Wilt

SHERRY MORRIS

When I first met Carol, I liked her immediately. She was warm and friendly and made me feel comfortable right away. I was new to the area and felt like an empty cup with no one to spend time with or to fill my days. But Carol quickly made me feel like I had found a fountain of friendship to help me make a new life in a strange city. What I discovered was an oasis to refresh my heart for years to come in a way I never expected.

As our friendship grew, she told me about a tragedy in her life that left me feeling sad and horrified. En route to a family reunion, Carol and her youngest daughter were following in a car behind her sister who was driving with Carol's three-year-old daughter, Janella, inside. My friend saw another car crash head-on into her sister's car. Her sister was killed at the scene. Janella was critically injured and died a week later. I was awed that Carol was not broken by the tragedy. Sad, yes. Wistful, yes. But devastated, no. Yet this tragedy had happened only a few months before I met her.

She talked about Janella often. Janella's memory was still very much alive in her mother's heart. Carol and I talked about the details of Janella's birth, when she learned to walk, how smart she was, what she liked to play with, and the funny things she said. On the first anniversary of Janella's death, I accompanied Carol to the grave where her little girl lay. I watched her other daughter and my own little girl run and play on the grassy knoll while Carol prayed. She never cried. Afterward, we went to lunch and she reminisced more about Janella, but she never became the melancholy and sad person I would have been if something that terrible had happened in my life.

Carol was my best friend. She and I spent many happy hours talking together over a plate of cookies or a pan of brownies. We attended the same church, went to Bible studies together, and had many friends in common. Our little girls played together happily. It was an idyllic time in my life. Having a close friend to spend time with allowed me to share the joys and challenges of being a young moth-

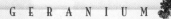

er. We also talked about God and our beliefs. Yet, through all the time I spent with her, I never really understood how she could be so calm about what must be the worst thing imaginable to happen in a mother's life. She seemed at peace with the tragedy, and her life reflected a calm assurance that in the scheme of things all was well.

Then, the day came when Carol's husband lost his job. He eventually found other work, but at a much lower rate of pay. Carol did not have a college degree or any particular skills, but she had a heart for people and she liked working with the elderly so she went to work in a nursing home. Though I knew she and her husband were struggling financially, I never knew that they were about to lose their home. When Carol told me about it, she stated it matter-of-factly. Without a trace of "poor me" or any anger about how unfair life was, she told me about their plans to move.

Not long after they moved to another town, my mother passed away. Carol drove some distance to my hometown for the funeral. It meant a lot to me that she came. Even though I was filled with great sorrow that my mother passed away so young, I remembered that my friend's child had only lived three years.

Like many who face grave reality in their lives, I faced a crisis of belief in my life when my mother died. I wondered, *How could God allow such unfair things to happen?* As each new wave of tumultuous emotion passed over me, I remember praying and crying out to God with my unanswered questions. Carol again came to my mind. She seemed to have no doubt that her daughter was already in a better place. When the next flame of adversity came along, she still didn't lose faith. Through both difficulties and sorrow, my friend always chose joy over sorrow and had peace in her heart. She did not just have head knowledge that God has a plan for each our lives, she had heart knowledge that it takes faith to overcome the pain of loss. Because she had both, she was able to keep a smile on her face and continue to reach out to others and love them without evidence of self-pity.

Though my friend still lives in another city and we don't see each other often, she has filled my cup with more than just friendship. Carol's childlike faith and steadfast endurance showed me that God gives peace to hearts that choose to believe in Him.

Friendships are only
possible when we open
the window of our heart
and allow the sunshine
of someone's life in.

A Golden Chain of Friendship

GINNY HOBSON

"Gin, I can't believe this is happening," Kathy said. We walked down the hallway of her house and passed picture after picture of her four boys. She had stopped to touch one of Brian, her oldest, and now he was gone. It seemed impossible. The boutonniere from his first prom was still fresh in the refrigerator. His room was just as he'd left it, and his bike was still in the front yard. Kathy moved with the motions of the living, but her heart was with her son. He had collapsed at school after a basketball game. He never woke up and died hours later from an undiagnosed, rare congenital heart defect.

Many times over the years I had seen Kathy face a crisis, but this one seemed to envelop us all. How did my strong friend survive? We had become friends in high school and I loved her honesty and quick wit. Everyone was her friend. When her parents moved away her senior year, my family offered her a bed and home for her last year of school which she gladly accepted. Rollers in the hair, homework marathons, and "boy talk" was our daily routine. I was amazed at her endurance in studying, helping at our house, and working at a store so she could contribute to her room and board.

She won enough votes that year to be a cheerleader, but the committee called back six hours later and said they'd made a mistake. She calmly said," Oh well, they miscounted," and took it in stride. How did she do that?

After we graduated, I got married, and Kathy went to nursing school. Then, I went to nursing school and Kathy got married. We were 1,000 miles apart, but with each birth of our children and event in our lives, we were there for each other in thoughts, prayers, calls, and letters. She, her husband, and her boys were always miles away from her family and friends, yet she established a loving, well-rooted home full of traditions and strong ties.

Once while we were visiting them in Virginia, Kathy received a call. Her father had died unexpectedly. He had faithfully given care to Kathy's mother who had been chronically ill for years. His heart just gave out. "I guess he was just tired," she said, "I wish I could have told him goodbye." Six weeks later her mother passed away and once again my brave friend took the grief in her life and weathered its storm with endurance.

But the strongest, most fierce storm of all was the loss of a child. Brian was our godchild. It seemed impossible when we heard the news, and we knew we had to come. To just be there was all I knew to do. Flowers and love poured in as teachers, parents, friends, and neighbors gave back the love they had known from Brian and his family. Food arrived from everywhere, and someone they didn't even know mowed their lawn. Moment by moment Kathy's strength of character become a light to us all. She wanted the funeral to focus on God's love, and all of Brian's friends were invited to their home.

Six months later I made a business trip to her area, and she wanted me to come and stay. I was concerned about how she would be so soon after Brian's death, wondering if our time understandably would be spent in grief. Instead, I was greeted by her warm smile, "I've got our time together all planned!"

She surprised me with a day at Williamsburg where we shopped and ate a wonderful dinner and talked nonstop and lovingly of Brian and all our children. There was sadness with the reality of loss, but the knowledge of his whereabouts was certain. Brian was gone from us for a time, but not forever. She then took us to a fun hotel where we talked all night like we were teenagers again and shared all we had gone through since high school. From where we started to where we were now was a long and winding path. The next day we shopped 'til we dropped. When I left, she gave me a most treasured gift to thank me for all I had meant to her over the years, when it was she that I admired so much. It was a beautiful gold bracelet with "#1 Friend" engraved on its front. I was surprised and overcome that my dear friend would honor me so. Her tenderness needed no words. I could feel both her pain and love all in one hug.

I will always cherish the lovely gold bracelet Kathy gave me. And when I remember Kathy, I will think of someone whose life is held together by a clasp of strength. Even when tested with fire, the clasp didn't break. Instead, she has remained strong and able to forge new links in the chain. Like the bracelet she gave me, Kathy will always be a treasure of my heart.

My Sunflower Friend

SHERRY MORRIS

A FRIEND who's a flower of sunshine

Is known for her listening and caring.

She drops loving deeds into withering hearts—

Seeds of thoughtfulness, kindness, and sharing.

Sometimes it's just with a look or a SMILE

That sends caring from her heart to mine.

Sometimes a sweet note is her way to say,

"Don't give up, you just keep on trying."

As a SUNFLOWER turns its face to the sun

And basks in the warmth of its glow,

I've looked in your heart, my sunflower friend,

And learned how a friendship can grow.

CHARACTER TRAIT
LOVE

To love and to be loved is to feel the sun from both sides.

No garden is complete without a sunflower friend. It is hard to be glum around these flowers of both happiness and caring. Those of us who plant a border of these tall, winsome flowers around the garden of our hearts soon find ourselves surrounded by a sanctuary of sunshine. Like a goldfinch delights in the seeds of the sunflower, we delight in the seeds of kindness and thoughtfulness that spill from the heart of a sunflower friend.

In the warm light of the friendly gesture we offer her, she turns her head toward us and begins to share the love and joy in her life—love and joy that come from a giving heart. Or, perhaps we don't notice this flower at all, until she surprises us with some deed we neither expect nor deserve. With a happy heart, a sunflower in our lives just seems to know the secret of giving without expecting much more than a smile in return.

It is to the sunflower friend that we look for encouragement. Just knowing that she cares helps us find the strength we need to keep on trying, Her loving ways are shown to us by the cards she sends just when we need a lift, the plans she makes for lunch during a difficult week, a small gift she quietly places on our desk when we thought no one remembered the occasion, or with just a hug because she thought we might be drooping. The sunflower friend listens with her heart and has the gift of knowing just the right way to respond. From the sunflower, we learn some of the most basic things about the seeds from which friendship grows—seeds of thoughtfulness, kindness, and caring. These are the seeds that fall from a sunflower's life so that we can carry them like a goldfinch to others.

THE CARE OF A SUNFLOWER FRIEND ~ *Remember to give back what you have received.*

Sunflower friends give and give so much that we often forget that they, too,
need the water of kindness, the nourishment of encouragement, and the fresh soil of giving.
These gifts of care and concern they so generously give to others are needed by them
as well. Remember to give back to your sunflower friend if they begin to wilt, because
they need you as much as you need them!

Kathy's Chair

SHERRY MORRIS

I had not worked at my job very long before I noticed something unusual about Kathy's office. Someone was always standing in her doorway chatting, eating pretzels from the jar she keeps on her desk, or sitting in her extra office chair. I knew she was warm and friendly, and she always has a smile on her face. I noticed, too, that she often brought gifts of homemade food and talked pleasantly with everyone, but I still didn't see why people spent so much time with her.

Maybe it's the pretzel jar, I thought to myself. *People like to have a snack now and then and will stop in to chat.* Then, one week she ran out of pretzels. So, I filled a candy dish for my desk. I did see a few more visitors, but the traffic in Kathy's doorway never even slowed down. *Maybe it's the chair,* I considered. So I placed a chair in my office and had a few people stop by, but never so many as Kathy.

Tongue in cheek though this story may be, I have learned about friendship by watching Kathy. Though tokens of friendship such as pretzels in a jar may be like a welcome mat in the doorway of the heart, it is the willingness to take time to listen and showing that you care that takes us from being acquaintances to being good friends.

As the weeks went by, I stopped trying to figure out Kathy's secret. I realized why our boss tolerates so much activity from Kathy's office. One day I was frustrated and angry over a situation I couldn't control, and was about to burst into tears. Kathy walked by and asked, "What's the matter?" Before I knew it, I found myself sitting in her chair sharing the whole story. She listened quietly, asked me lots of questions, offered me advice based on wisdom, and then prayed with me. I left her office feeling much better. Since that day, I've been back many times. In fact, the day just doesn't get off to a good start unless I've spent a little time with Kathy.

Kathy is our financial secretary, but I know that my friend has a larger role to play. Besides keeping the numbers straight, she helps keep lives in order, too. Treating others with kindness is always her first priority. She is a sounding board and a listening ear. People respond to her kind words and hugs and the many things she does for others. She is loved by all. I have learned many secrets of friendship while sitting in Kathy's chair.

A Sunflower in My Garden

DENISE ROUNDS

Of my friends, one stands out as a sunflower friend. In fact, she gave me a start of sunflowers that fill a whole flowerbed in my backyard. My friend Sharon loves gardening and art. Years ago, we met as we planned crafts for a vacation Bible school. I was drawn to her ready smile, her politeness, and her courteous manner. She was a true picture of a gracious, southern lady.

A few years later we became walking buddies. We would meet at her curb for "walk talks" and share our joys, prayers, hopes, and dreams. She taught me the ways to grow the plants we saw as we walked. And she showed me genuine hospitality with plates of home-baked cookies, plant cuttings, and bunches of flowers that were dropped off by her smiling boys at my front door.

Two years ago she and her family were transplanted to California. Her move has brought changes in our friendship, yet it has not dimmed the delight we still experience when we hear from one another. Frequently we send or receive cards or packages with notes attached that say "I had to buy this for you." And our e-mails are like our long "walk talks" of the past.

Not long ago Sharon was in town. Her mother was awaiting a serious surgery. Sharon greeted me with a warm hug as soon as she saw me and asked all about my family. I answered, "Sharon, this visit is about you and your mother!" I asked them how they were coping. They answered honestly, but with great hope. They were amazed at how kind the hospital staff and physicians were to them. I didn't find that odd. A sunflower friend lights up the lives of others, who can't help but respond in kind.

From the wreath on my front door to the hospitality I practice inside my home, I see how my sunflower friend has touched my life. Her generous and caring spirit has brought beauty and joy to me. She has been a bright spot in my garden, like the sunflowers she gave me that bloom every year just outside my window.

A Lesson in Giving

GINNY HOBSON

Carrie always has a smile for you no matter what the day. And she laughs so much at herself that it makes it easy to be around her. Everyone just loves her honest, practical way of looking at life. She has a way of making everyone feel important and part of the team.

I met Carrie in the bleachers at the baseball field when our sons were eight years old. She always looked so polished and rested and would share her stories that would have us all in stitches. Over the years, she never missed a game, homeroom party, or school event, and each teacher knew who to thank for their often-received gifts of love. The rest of us moms would look on with admiration and wonder at how she did it.

It wasn't till years later when she and I began working together that I learned her secret of success. She put others first—what a concept! I certainly had never seen anyone do that before, but over and over I saw this sunflower brighten people's days with her thoughtfulness: cookies baked, birthdays never missed, cards, letters of encouragement, and a smile or hug whenever it was needed.

In the small business where we worked, the pressure was always on. Missed deadlines, who-did-this blame games, and I-don't-care attitudes abounded. Those of us who worked together felt like we were always in a pressure vise. But Carrie touched every person's life with her giving spirit. The years went by, and we all learned to slow down a moment and smell the flowers as Carrie would share a funny story. She had a way of capturing in her heart the essence of joy and giving it to you in her smile, her laughter, and descriptions. No longer did we scrap at each other. It happened without us noticing, but we all began to change. Where there once were scowls, smiles bloomed. Carrie helped us schedule and plan, and always taught us to

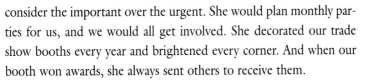

consider the important over the urgent. She would plan monthly parties for us, and we would all get involved. She decorated our trade show booths every year and brightened every corner. And when our booth won awards, she always sent others to receive them.

The more she gave, the more she taught us and the more we loved her. Many a personal problem was solved in her office though no counseling fee was paid—just love and honesty were shared, hugs and smiles with the encouragement that "you can do it." If there was a major decision to be made, we would say, "go ask Carrie." If it was the wrong thing to do, her heart would tell us. Carrie spent countless extra hours making our lives easier by planning activities, picking up a ball we'd dropped, or filling a void we hadn't even discovered yet.

Then one day her sunshine began to dim. We didn't see it flicker at first. Her eyes would glaze, and her laughter lessened. She became more quiet and distant. Our sunflower was wilting. Her days of lifting us up had drained her strength. It was time for us to give sunshine back to our friend. Two weeks' vacation was ordered by management. Her birthday came, and this time she was on the receiving end. Friends and coworkers sent her cards galore, smiles, hugs, and encouraging words. Her department divided the extra responsibilities that she had taken on for all of us.

Owners, managers, and the entire staff resoundingly agreed to preserve Carrie at all cost. Our "sunflower and day-brightener" was just too important. To have a friend who gives and gives is a wonderful gift indeed, but we all learned and now remember that a sunflower friend sometimes needs a little sunshine of her own.

My Rose Friend

SHERRY MORRIS

My FRIEND, you are a rose to me—
A flower that is priceless and dear.
You brighten my days with your giving ways
And add color to each passing year.

Like a ROSE as it blooms, unfolds slowly
Whether in sunshine or in the rain,
You've opened your heart through life's blessings
And shared both my joy and my pain.

Like a ROSE with a thorned, briared stem,
You know how to cut to the truth,
And even when giving a well-deserved prick,
A rose has a fragrance to soothe.

My FRIEND, you are a great blessing to me,
A reflection of nature's best art.
Like the rose is esteemed in the garden,
You're a treasure and jewel in my heart.

CHARACTER TRAIT
FAITHFULNESS

A true friend is a treasure of the heart.

The friend who is a rose in our lives offers us the deepest and most beautiful kind of friendship. Through both joy and sorrow, she adds rich color to our lives. No matter how many years or miles we are apart, a closeness and bond of friendship with a rose friend spans both time and distance. The trust we place in her brings to our lives a special fragrance that we know will remain with us always. The rose is perhaps the truest of all friendships, and we each desire to have one with whom to share the special moments and memories of our lives.

Roses come in many varieties. From pure white to the deepest red, the true colors of a rose friend in our lives are also as varied as we need them to be. Their faithfulness is what makes them so valuable to us. Come what may, a rose friendship blooms forever.

The rose, even though it is beautiful, has thorns on its stems that often prick our hearts with honesty, prune us with gentle reminders to keep our lives well-rooted in the things that really matter, and poke us as needed with the truth about who we are. The painful truth may leave us bleeding, but her unconditional love is soothing and often makes us stronger and wiser in the days to come. Like the rose in a garden, a rose friend is an esteemed and valued flower in the garden of the heart.

THE CARE OF A ROSE FRIEND *Always treasure the rose.*

Rose friends need to know our friendship is unconditional and that their truthfulness is received without fear of rejection. They also need to know we hold dear their faithfulness and do not take them for granted. Remember rose friends are the true friends who will see you through whatever life may bring. A smile from this friend is assurance that you have a friend forever.

The Prickly Rose

GINNY HOBSON

Terry and I have been friends for more than sixteen years. She's a prickly rose friend. I say "prickly" because Terry always tells me the truth before she tells me anything else. When I am down and out or up then down, she always reminds me where center is, and it's not on me. She makes me roll my cares onto God and quit thinking of myself. And I do the same for her. In fact, we have become so accountable to each other that if we have been especially irritated with our families, we just don't call each other. Because if we complain or tell our side of the story, the other will say things like, "Did you pray about it?" or "What did he really say?" For years, we've tried to complain to each other to no avail.

One time I didn't call her for two weeks and when I finally did she asked, "Why haven't you called me?"

"Because I didn't want to."

"Oh, are you ready to talk about it?" she inquired calmly, not knowing what "it" was all about.

"No," I answered resoundingly.

She flashed back, "Then why are you calling me?"

"Because I think I might want to talk about it," I half-heartedly replied, and then we would begin, she giving me the same challenges I so often gave to her—set boundaries then let go, forgive, try harder, look at the other person's side, pray and then pray some more.

To have a true friend to be accountable with is a very special gift, and one I have truly valued. Through the years, Terry and I have discussed and decided that there is no such thing as a "functional family." We all have some dysfunction somewhere; otherwise we wouldn't really need God to help us "function." With that conclusion, we have felt very comfortable being honest with each other and accountable as friends.

One day she called me and said with a flat depressed tone, "Dino bought the Chevy Blazer today."

I replied, "Great, but you don't sound too excited. Isn't that what you wanted—a new Chevy Blazer to replace the old one you sold?"

"You don't understand," she said, "He bought the old one."

"Again?" I asked, "Isn't this the second time he's bought it back?"

"He loves it," she said defeatedly.

Trying hard not to laugh, I pointed out all the wonderful attributes of owning a twenty-year-old bucket of bolts and reminded her how much we loved watching *Home Improvement* together, because we both have a "Tim" at home. Arr... Arr... Arr!

No matter how large or small the difficulty, once again we would help each other overcome our "want to get even," or "I'm furious over this," reaction to whatever life brings. Knowing that I'm not going to get any sympathy with Terry—not even whining produces sympathy or empathy to my complaints—often makes me realize it's not worth the effort in reporting to her my latest frustration. Because the heart of a true friend, like Terry, always tells the truth; and though it may sometimes hurt, the wound often results in a teachable spirit that learns to depend on God. Like iron sharpens iron and makes it a more useful tool, a true friend is someone who helps us become stronger in the Lord.

A Rose Named Dixie

CAROLYN MARBERGER

The sweetest fragrance of friendship for me came at a bittersweet time in my life. My husband, my lover, my companion, and my best friend for more than thirty years was dying. Many friends came to express their sorrow and concern for us. One special friend, however, spoke love without saying much at all. While sitting in the waiting room during one of many hospital visits and feeling that I just couldn't cope, I would look up to see her smiling face and feel her comforting hugs. Somehow she knew when I was alone and that I needed her during those difficult weeks.

We did not have insurance to cover a catastrophic illness. I needed to be at my husband's side; I could not work. Quietly, throughout the whole ordeal, my friend somehow arranged for our rent to be paid. I loved and appreciated her so much for this gift, but it was just knowing she was there for me that meant the most—crying and laughing with me as we remembered the funny things, and saying nothing when words were just too empty.

The day came all too soon and my husband went home to heaven. Without a word, my friend saw to it that my house was prepared for soon-to-arrive family and friends—cleaning, doing laundry, stocking pantry shelves, and even strategically placing boxes of tissues around my house. She met my needs even before I knew what they were.

In the sad weeks that followed, she allowed me to grieve, sometimes leaving me alone and sometimes staying at my side. She had lost her husband just a few years before, and standing with me now was like reliving her loss all over again. Yet my friend did so willingly, with thoughtful compassion.

Shakespeare wisely said, "A rose by any other name would smell as sweet." The rose has been a symbol for many things down through the ages. But in my life, the rose is a symbol for friendship, and my rose has a name. The fragrance of friendship she has brought into to my life sweetened the most bitter kind of hurt I've ever experienced, and I will always be grateful for a rose named Dixie.

Through It All

G I N N Y   H O B S O N

Linda is as true a rose friend as a woman could ever be, and she helped me through one of the most difficult times in my life—the "letting go" of my daughter.

Linda and I met when our boys were ten years old. She is tall and I am short. She was always in perfect order, on time, and came prepared; while I was usually late, had forgotten my purse, and was flustered.

Through hours of ball games, time at the local swimming pool, and school outings, we became good friends. She was a rose friend with such gentle thorns that when she gave her advice, I often didn't notice the pain until later. While rationalizing my feelings or actions, I'd then remember a comment or question Linda had said that would cause me to stop and reexamine my heart. When Linda and her husband eventually moved away, I would often call her for her true rose counsel.

My daughter Jennifer's "love of her life" was a nice looking young man named David. I was sure he was not ready for marriage. He just didn't seem to us to be as "perfect" for my daughter as she thought he was. I discussed in lengthy detail my objections to Linda, pointing out all his imperfections.

"Don't you think he's just young and in love?" Linda said.

"Young and in love," I repeated doubtfully. "I'm sure he's not ready!"

Then, she gave me her true rose observation along with an "all is well" smile. "He does seem to have the qualities to make a good husband and father."

Huh? I thought.

Later, I began thinking about this "young and in love" concept. I listed all his faults one by one on my grade card: monopolizes Jennifer's time, doesn't come excitedly to our family functions (I couldn't imagine why not), and doesn't talk to us that much (again, why?). Somehow my list was shorter than I thought. And then I realized Linda was right; he did have a great love and care for my daughter, a deep faith in God, an excellent job, was responsible, thrifty, and loved children. How did she see all that I had missed? I finally resolved to let go and within weeks, they were engaged. They truly were a couple in love and planned their wedding with great excitement.

Linda came to help the week of the wedding. And anything that could have gone wrong did. My husband's grandmother flew down the same day and within one hour of arrival fell down in our yard, shattered her shoulder, and fractured her arm. Linda added Grandma to the top of her list. Our plan for the week before the wedding was full of errands, lunches out, and time for rest—all of which were delayed, rearranged, and forgotten due to lengthy doctor's appointments and x-rays needed for Grandma. We were blessed that the damage was not permanent, but the time lost was! Linda pressed clothes, answered phones, cooked meals, coordinated relatives, baby-sat my youngest child, and tried to help me to stay calm. I couldn't have done it without her.

The wedding day included last minute errands, lunch, then home for a rest. All the bridesmaids' dresses and mine were at the church. Our schedule was already overloaded when my daughter said, "We forgot the unity candle!" Of course, it was on the Wednesday "to do" list that was forgotten while we were at the doctor with Grandma. We still had to pick up the wedding dress, Jennifer's shoes, and two flower arrangements. By the time we arrived at the church, we were late and never returned home for our rest. As my son escorted me down the aisle, I saw my sweet friend smile at me, still dressed in her denim jumper! She never had the chance to go home and change clothes.

The next day Linda helped me get ready for a brunch for thirty family members and friends. She worked quietly and quickly, then left for the airport only to find her flight in Chicago was canceled. She spent the whole day and night in the airport. Greater love has no woman than she who lays down to sleep in an airport for a friend! And she never even told me about it. I found out from her husband six months later. She had done it all from her heart, and her self-sacrifice was never mentioned.

When she calls today, she always says brightly, "Hello, Mrs. Hobson," and I respond, "Well, hello, Mrs. Judkins," and she lifts my spirits with her understanding voice. Then we talk as if there are no miles between us and it's just been a minute or two since we've shared our hearts.

My Faithful Rose

LORENE HOPKINS, SHERRY MORRIS, & GINNY HOBSON

How deep are the roots of the beautiful ROSE?

How wonderful and unchanging its fragrance.

How lovely the bough that brings forth each year

The flower that my heart embraces.

The roots of the ROSE grow as deep as her heart,

Her fragrance is as sweet as her presence.

The rose, like a friend, grows strong through the years;

Faithfulness is ever her essence.

How true and how lovely is the beautiful ROSE?

Like the poets have extolled through the ages—

When bouquets are picked from the garden of life,

It's the rose that's most dear on life's pages.

To Have and Be a Friend

LAUREL YOUNG

My friendship with Cynthia was slow to bloom and grow, although it was something I had wanted for twenty years. I truly believe that God gave me the desire to cultivate the sisterly relationship we have because He knew what a blessing Cynthia would be in my life.

Long before Cynthia and I got to know each other, I admired her dark Lebanese beauty, erect dignified posture, and deep calm voice. With these attributes she conveyed intelligence, wisdom, and authority when she spoke. People listened to her and trusted her. I was attracted to her as one is to a lovely crimson rose on a slender statuesque stem, but her prickly qualities of insight and candor kept me at a distance. I was afraid of how she might use these traits with me.

Years later when Cynthia and I were drawn together by concern for a mutual friend, I learned to value her gift of discernment. She understands my deepest feelings and motives and helps me to see them from God's point of view, whether I want to or not. She has influenced me to pray my way out of negative feelings about myself and others without being critical of me or them. When she prays, her words seem to touch on all the most pertinent facts surrounding the situa-

tion and during that very process God shows me the direction He wants me to take. In this way, Cynthia meets the most important criteria of a good friend—she leads me close to God.

The rose is an amazing flower that can grow and give pleasure almost everywhere in the world. Cynthia's friendship reminds me of this because her thoughtfulness touches the hearts of all who know her. She instinctively knows when to pick up the phone to see how I am or to offer help. When my father died recently, she not only brought me and my family a delicious home-cooked meal to ease my burden, she sent my mother who lives in Oregon (and whom she had never met) a sincerely caring note. These acts were especially appreciated because much of her time was consumed with commuting between Memphis and Little Rock to attend to the needs of her own parents who are ill.

I cannot count the number of times she has dropped everything she was doing during her busy day just to pick up the phone to give me a word of encouragement, to kindly urge me to take better care of myself, or to invite me to go "walk and talk" when she senses that I am in need of a friend. She offers to look after my teenage son so my husband and I can have a weekend getaway. She always makes me feel appreciated by encouraging me in my work and sending me heartfelt loving thank you notes for special gifts and favors. But I am not the only one she reaches out to. She faithfully sends money to help a needy friend, comforts and prays with friends undergoing the ravages of illness, and recently organized a collection to help the victims of a fire that destroyed their home. Never have I met a person who so consistently makes time to reach out to others and puts their needs ahead of her own.

I cherish Cynthia for all these things, but most of all because she makes me feel like I am an important part of her life as well. I am deeply complimented that she trusts me with her concerns and allows me the opportunity to reciprocate with her for her many kindnesses. When I first made a determined effort not just to have Cynthia as a friend, but to be a friend, her habitual unselfishness made it difficult for her to even talk about her needs and problems. But she now makes me feel as though I have as much to give her as she gives to me. The great love and respect that I feel for her makes me treasure this relationship. I intend to nurture it as I would the most prized rose in my garden.

My Pressed Flower Friend

SHERRY MORRIS

In my book of memories there is

A pressed FLOWER that fills a page,

With a gentle fragrance lingering still,

Though it's faded now with age.

The way my FRIEND smiled and laughed,

The many ways she cared,

Are a legacy that she left behind

In stories I love to share.

So remember the hearts who've touched your life.

It's what we each are here for.

A pressed FLOWER gently reminds us

To love and treasure our friendships more.

DEAR FRIENDS NOW GONE

Time endures but cannot fade the memories that love has made.

Some friends remain in our lives only in spirit and through our memories. The love and joy these flowers of friendship gave us are dried and carefully preserved to forever capture their color, beauty, and sweet aroma. A pressed flower friend may have overcome great difficulty or stood bravely through the winds of life before they left us. Long after they are gone, their lives remain an inspiration to our hearts. Sometimes an event brings the pressed flower friend to mind, and our hearts are carried back to another time and place when this flower was a part of our lives. We smell the sweetness of their memory as a song is played or a story is told. The memory of these friendships lasts a lifetime like pressed flowers in a book, on a special page, in the garden of our hearts.

THE CARE OF A PRESSED FLOWER FRIEND

Share the memories.

Though pressed flowers are gone from our lives, their families often remain. If we take the time to call or send a note to these loved ones, we let them know how much this friend has meant to our lives. It is often a comfort and a joy to know that the memory of their loved one still lives on in the heart of another.

Also, remember that none of us know what tomorrow may bring. Every day is an opportunity to love and care for each friend who is living and growing in the garden of your heart.

A Photo on My Windowsill

GLYNDA TURLEY

(as told to Sherry Morris and Ginny Hobson)
Glynda Turley's art graces the pages of this book.

On my kitchen windowsill sits a photo of my friend Sherry. Every morning,
I look at her smile and remember how she lived. I met her through my daughter, Shannon,
and quickly appreciated her gentle wit, quiet charm, and deep compassion.

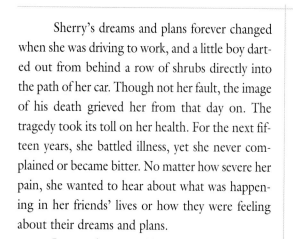

Sherry's dreams and plans forever changed when she was driving to work, and a little boy darted out from behind a row of shrubs directly into the path of her car. Though not her fault, the image of his death grieved her from that day on. The tragedy took its toll on her health. For the next fifteen years, she battled illness, yet she never complained or became bitter. No matter how severe her pain, she wanted to hear about what was happening in her friends' lives or how they were feeling about their dreams and plans.

I remember a troubled time when I needed Sherry. As an artist, I paint for a living. The pressure of needing to create left me feeling like I couldn't cope with the workload. I was having anxiety attacks. Sherry knew I was struggling, so she began calling me almost daily. I would try to tell her that my troubles didn't rate at all compared to everything she was going through. She would say that my pain was real, and it hurt just like hers did. Unlike me, my friend never had time for dwelling on things she couldn't change in her life. She was too busy thinking about what she could do to bless and encourage others.

Sherry is a special flower in the garden of my heart. Like roots that go deep into the soil to find needed moisture, Sherry dug in and found what she needed to live with a happy heart. Showered by the love of her friends, Sherry stood her ground and thrived. When she finally went to join God in Heaven, I believe that the little boy whose life ended so tragically was there to greet her. I think that Sherry gives him now what she gave to us while she was here—the gift of her unselfish love.

In gathering flowers in my garden, Sherry will always be forever pressed in the pages of my heart. In a way, the photo on my windowsill is like a pressed flower. From Sherry, I learned so much— patience to overcome, how to encourage, and thoughtfulness. These are still growing in my life, and I want to plant them in the hearts of others.

A
friend loveth
at
all times
* * *
Proverbs 17:17
KJV

Holy Bible

A Pair of Skates, a Broken Arm, and a Steadfast Friend

VIRGINIA BRADFIELD

As I looked out our living room window on a sunny Saturday afternoon, I could see my two daughters, ages ten and thirteen, playing with a new little girl in our neighborhood. Laughing and giggling, my girls put a pair of roller skates on their new friend and were teaching her how to skate down our rather steep driveway. I hadn't met her yet, but I could tell just by looking that the girls had already become fast friends.

I was relaxing with a good book on a rare Saturday afternoon with nothing I had to do. My husband was watching a game on TV. All of a sudden I heard a yell. "Mom, I think Mitzi broke her arm." As the girls piled into the door, I looked at Mitzi's bulging skin and knew immediately that her arm was broken. Though Mitzi was obviously in great pain, this ten-year-old only gave a whimper as my husband gently picked her up and carried her down the street to her house. My girls and I followed.

We walked into Mitzi's yard just as the moving van that delivered furniture to the house was driving away. We were greeted at the door by Mitzi's father and a room full of unpacked boxes. I thought, *Welcome to the neighborhood*, as my husband handed him his daughter instead of a plate of cookies. We felt terrible, and I guess it showed. Mitzi's dad calmly said he would take his daughter to the hospital. My husband went to help, but I stayed behind and went in the house to talk to Mitzi's mom.

Looking into the den I saw Mitzi's mother, Lee, surrounded by chaos everywhere and sitting on a box nursing her three-month-old son. She was an extremely beautiful woman with big blue eyes, coal black hair, and a bright sunny smile. I sheepishly introduced myself and my girls and explained further what had happened. Lee put me at ease, laughed, and said she understood. My relief was great, and her gracious spirit was evident as she offered me a cool drink. When the two men returned with Mitzi, her arm was in a big cast. The girls went into Mitzi's room to visit and to play, and Lee and I began a friendship that has transcended time.

Over the next few years we shared coffee, walks, neighborhood news, and the pain of divorce in both our lives, a year apart. We became single parents who each strived to maintain a stable family life for our children. With the trauma of divorce, we leaned heavily on each other for emotional support to cope with all the problems faced by single moms. We developed a rapport with each other that few friends ever experience. It was Lee's radiant personality that helped me through this difficult period of my life.

Lee and I both reached the point of feeling ready to date again at about the same time. We were both cautious and insecure but open to what God might have in store. One day Lee called and said, "I met this wonderful man today. He asked me out, but I think he's perfect for you. He's a teacher and is raising his three children by himself. I gave him your phone number."

"Lee," I said in surprise, "you didn't!" But four months later I married the dear and kind man my friend had picked for me. Lee fell in love with a well-respected doctor who took her away from a life of just scraping by. What he gave her instead was a comfortable life and love for her children.

One day, Lee called me and said that she had noticed a lump in her breast. She and her husband decided to go to Houston for diagnosis and treatment. Through the efforts of her husband and the best care money could buy, Lee lived eight more years. Looking young and still so beautiful, she died at age fifty-four.

Though several years have now past, I still miss her beautiful smile, contagious laugh, practical spirit, and sincere loyalty as a friend. Lee's daughter, Mitzi, now works as an accountant with my daughter. The two of them are still fast friends, only now Mitzi and Ginny "put on skates" together to ride over the ups and downs of cash flow. I can still see Lee's beautiful smile when I look at Mitzi and hear her in Mitzi's voice. Then I remember back to the day when a broken arm on a ten-year-old child brought me together with my dear and eternal friend.

With Love, from Carrie

CARRIE BARNES

Dear Dawna,

Friend of my heart, I miss you! Do you remember when we first met in the church parking lot more than twenty years ago? You were so beautiful when you walked up to me and said, "The Lord told me to take care of your children one day each month so that you can attend women's luncheons at church." I was startled by your offer, but being new to Tulsa and not having anyone to leave my children with, I decided to say yes to your offer. Little did I realize that would be the beginning of our beautiful friendship. My children absolutely adored you. They could hardly wait to be with you.

Dawna, you taught me to savor the moments and celebrate every season. You introduced me to the wonderful preparation time of Advent and the celebration of Epiphany. I learned from you to decorate my home for every season and to teach my children about family and traditions. I remember the vacation we shared with your family at your cabin in Colorado. I treasure the walks we took to the meadow to look for elk and deer. Just sitting quietly on the deck and reading a book was a tender time. We laughed, hiked, played, and loved being together as two families.

How often did I come home to find a small gift you left on my porch, or a card of encouragement in my mailbox from you? You taught me how to be a friend as I watched you love your friends. You shared so many secrets about childrearing and marriage that have helped me all my life. I watched carefully, because I know what fine young men your sons have become. I watched you live each day and treat your husband with such tender affection. You truly were a Proverbs 31 woman and a witness of God's love.

On the day you came by to tell me you were to have surgery, we cried together as the doctor told you, "It's cancer." We prayed as you fought to live. My heart was absolutely broken that August when you left us. How could this be? Dawna, my friend, my counselor, you went to be with God. Even though it has been more than ten years now, I still miss you. You will be always be in my heart.

I love you forever,

Carrie

My Mother's Friend

DEE TABOR

She was my mother's friend more than my own. But like an annual flower comes back each spring to a garden, my memories of Mary Hastings have returned through the years whenever I think of friendship. I recall her kind, pleasant manner and her laugh, and most importantly, the sacrifices she made to help our family.

It was in the year 1950 on a bitter cold January night when my youngest brother decided to make his debut in this world. There was a solid sheet of ice on the road. Dad had gone into town to get the doctor, but hadn't made it back yet. Frightened and concerned for our mother, I frantically climbed the steep hill to Mary's house. Mary came willingly to help, though she had to brave the cold night air on foot and slide all the way to our home. Long before the doctor arrived, Mary delivered my baby brother. His color wasn't right, and he didn't cry so she gave him a slap, then cut and tied the umbilical cord. Afterward, Mama let us kids gather around her bedside to get a glimpse of our beautiful and healthy baby brother. We all rejoiced together for our new addition and for Mama's friend who cared enough to come and help in our time of need.

Two years later Mary again came to our family's aid. A telegram arrived bearing sad news. My sister's husband had been badly burned in an accident and had died. I know my sister felt so alone with two small children and most of her family living so far away. Our family was large and money was scarce, so it was impossible to travel when we wanted, much less when it was necessary. Though Mary's family was as poor as our own, I remember the day she came to our house and placed what may have been her family's entire savings into my mother's hand. Mary simply said, "Go and be with your daughter." Her words and actions spoke volumes to me about the meaning of true friendship.

Although more than forty years have passed since I have seen or talked with my mother's friend, I have never forgotten her. She has been an example to me and has taught me a valuable lesson about what being a good friend and neighbor are all about. Time and again I have been reminded of her unselfish acts of kindness toward our family. Even though I was only a little girl when I knew her, I would like her to know that the way she lived those many years ago touched my heart and made a difference to me and my family.

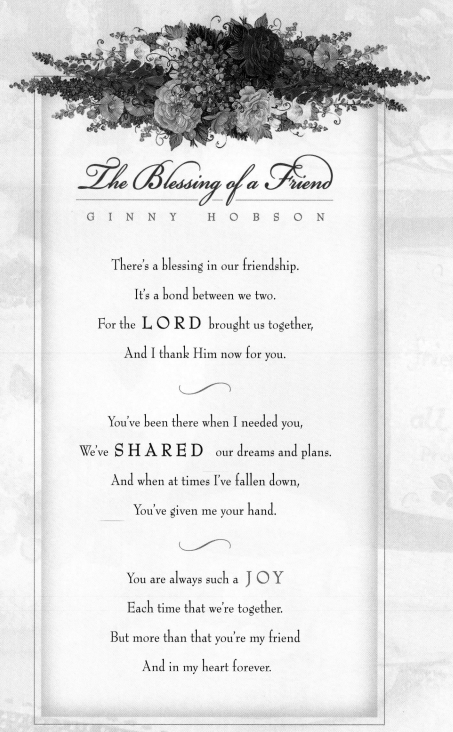

The Blessing of a Friend

GINNY HOBSON

There's a blessing in our friendship.

It's a bond between we two.

For the **LORD** brought us together,

And I thank Him now for you.

You've been there when I needed you,

We've **SHARED** our dreams and plans.

And when at times I've fallen down,

You've given me your hand.

You are always such a **JOY**

Each time that we're together.

But more than that you're my friend

And in my heart forever.

A BOUQUET OF FRIENDSHIP

Friendships are gathered and tied with heartstrings.

A basket, gardening shears, and a pair of gloves are the tools the gardener uses to gather a bouquet for her table. Strolling among the flowers, there are many to choose from. These are carefully snipped and given a place of prominence for the gardener to enjoy. Maybe it's the color that delights her eye. Maybe it's an occasion that a certain flower brings to memory.

Like the gardener, come gather the tools of friendship and step into the garden of the heart. As we consider the many kinds of flowers in our lives, we can gather a bouquet of people who are special to our lives. What makes them dear to us? The wildflower, the rose, the tulip, and the many others are snipped and arranged into a heart.

Just as a gardener walks among the flowers in the garden, each of us should take the time to stroll in the garden of friendship and see what is growing. Pruning shears are needed to cut away weeds of bitterness that may have taken root. The gardener's gloves of forgiveness gently pull the weeds so as not to damage the flower. As we open our eyes to the many kinds of flowers in our lives, our appreciation for each individual flower grows. Yet, gathered together and tied with heartstrings, they add a beauty that is not found anywhere else. Each bouquet of friendship is uniquely our own.

While friends are near us, we feel that all is well.
Our everyday life blossoms
suddenly into bright possibilities.

— HELEN KELLER

A friend is a push when you've stopped . . .

A word when you're lonely . . .

A guide when you're searching . . .

A smile when you're sad . . .

A song when you're glad.

A Circle of Friends

CINDY PERRYMAN

This story is not about one particular friend, but a group of very dear friends who have stood with me during some very difficult times. When trying circumstances come knocking at the door of our lives, sometimes it takes more than just our family to keep us going. Like a wreath of flowers hung on a door, my friends represent many kinds of flowers in my life who form a circle of protection and caring around my heart. I will always be thankful for each of them.

I had just gone to work full time when I began to feel ill. The doctor prescribed some medication and recommended further tests if I didn't see any improvement. I didn't feel any better, but concern about my symptoms was quickly put aside when two of my daughters were involved in a serious car accident.

Sheila, age sixteen, was driving and lost control of her car. She hit a tree, and both her legs were broken. Stephanie, who was thirteen, shattered her left arm. My husband, Mike, and I were driving to church when we came upon the scene shortly after it happened. With our hearts in our throats, we sent word to our family and friends, who responded in so many ways we will not soon forget.

The crowd who prayed for our daughters in the emergency room lent support as Sheila underwent surgery and had a steel rod inserted in each leg. They rejoiced with us when Stephanie was treated for two broken bones and released. Sheila remained in the hospital for a week; she would need a great deal of assistance for some time. My special friends touched our lives through visits, phone calls, prayers, and so much more. Tommye brought snack food to us every day; JoDell sat with Sheila so that I could go home to shower and get some rest.

Connie, Cheryl, Angie, and Pam visited often and offered any assistance they could give. Paula arranged for and delivered meals to my family. When we brought Sheila home a week later, my circle of friends rallied together to again provide meals and do my housecleaning. People arrived at our door with rehabilitation equipment they had borrowed and words of encouragement.

After weeks of God's provision for our needs through my many dear friends, we resumed a semi-normal life with Sheila in physical therapy three times a week. I had been too involved in my children's lives to give attention to the pain I was experiencing. But it had increased measurably during the ordeal, so I made another appointment to see a doctor. He suggested an MRI, and I waited for the results. It was not good news. Further testing confirmed I had multiple sclerosis.

It was quite a shock. I was overwhelmed. But once more, my family and my friends gathered to surround me with the protection and caring that have helped me make the adjustments in my life I've had to make. It had only been two months since the car accident, yet my friends again took up my burdens and carried them for me. Each of my friends is a different flower in a wreath that I will always keep at the door of my heart.

Tommye, my ROSE, just wouldn't let me
give up. She pricked me with honest encouragement
and told me God wasn't finished with me yet.

Pam, my LILAC, came to let me cry on her
shoulder and offered me hope through her words
that I knew to be spiritually sound.

Paula, my WILDFLOWER, made me
laugh with her funny ways of making the ordinary
amusing.

Cheryl, a TULIP, whose daughter is also my
youngest daughter's best friend, fills a gap
in my life like no one else ever could.

Connie, the encouraging SUNFLOWER
in my life, seemed to know just when
to pick up the phone and call.

JoDell and *Angie,* my GERANIUMS,
are overcomers who taught me to keep going
so my life can be blessed as theirs have been.

Cheryl and Angie paid for my house to be cleaned for several weeks. Paula came to fix meals and
did our laundry on the days when I was just too tired and sick to take care of even the smallest things.
My other friends called with words of encouragement and offered much-needed prayers. Although this has
been one of the most difficult times in my life, I thank God for my circle of friends who have helped
me carry the load. Each one of them will always be a treasure in the garden of my heart.

A Bouquet for Ginny & Sherry

GINNY HOBSON & SHERRY MORRIS

Opening the gate to our garden of friendship is a joyful task. We try to step inside and visit this special place in our lives every day. The busyness of work schedules and the time needed to be wives and mothers sometimes interferes with spending time with a friend,  but taking time for friendship is often just the refreshment and encouragement needed to give us new energy. Friendship has been described in scripture as "a sheltering tree." Like trees provide needed shelter, friends are a hedge of joy in the good times and pro-tection in the not-so-good times. Both Ginny and Sherry have a garden that is flowering with many friends.

There are two roses that stand tall above the rest. One is Sherry's sister, Cindy; the other is Ginny's sister, Cindy. Yes you read "Cindy" twice. Cindy Kay is Sherry's sister. Cindy #2 is Ginny's sister. We all became one family when our parents married—Ginny's mom to Sherry's dad. The four of us girls have shared buds of true rose friendship that have grown into full flower through the years.

Ginny's Bouquet

As I look at my garden, I see flowers of every color, a rainbow of friends. My life has been made fresh and alive with the laughter and support of friends like Carrie, Kathy, Linda, Terry, Mitzi, Jane, and so many others. There are always new flowers being planted by the Master Gardener, and I will discover them in the years to come.

Can a wildflower be an attorney? Karen is both. Imagine the combination. Whenever I look at something in the store she says, "Get it. You deserve it." A true wildflower, her "verdict" is that her friends should have fun. She's a blessing in my life.

Rosalind is the truest rose you could ever find. Her care and concern for each of her friends is unconditional. She challenges us with life's truths and keeps us focused on what is important. She has become a renowned sculptor and travels extensively, yet she never forgets an event in our family's lives. She is always ready for spontaneous fun: "Let's all learn to scuba dive!" I don't like fish on the end of a hook much less having one swimming next to me, but scuba dive we did. Rosalind always has a thoughtful heart and is my kindred spirit. We share our creative endeavors—hers, sculpture; and mine, art. We share our husband's love of flying in small planes. They talk and laugh at the wind, while we hold hands and pray. We share the love of our God and our families.

Sherry is a steadfast geranium friend whose strength of heart and sincerity in life is refreshing. Her focus is the eternal issues of the heart. Through the loss of her mother and husband's acute illness, Sherry has been an example to look up to for she has never lost heart or her faith.

Then there is Kathy, a wildflower through and through. Her smile is uplifting and her laugh is infectious. Whatever the situation, she finds the humor in it, and soon we are all giggling like little girls. At restaurants, are women in their forties supposed to act like teenagers? With Kathy, we do!

Janie is a wonderful sunflower friend. She has four children at home and manages rental properties, yet somehow she finds the time to be with her friends. A true sunflower, when she has a party she doesn't leave anyone out and invites 100 plus! Then she serves, acts as hostess, cooks, and cleans for those she loves.

Sherry's Bouquet

Arranging my bouquet of friendship in my mind and heart is a joy. Because I work as a children's minister, I have had the privilege of making friends who share many heart-satisfying moments with me. Together we touch children's lives through games and stories and hugs and music and more. We touch one another's hearts with encouragement and camaraderie and the support that comes from understanding the joys and frustrations of being a part of a child's life. I have both given and received a healing hug from Mary and Trish when the best laid plans went awry. But I have also shared happy tears with Sandie and Karen as we watched a "shy" child sing a solo for the first time during a Christmas pageant. Frances, Vicki, Molly, April, Sonia, and Pam have shared the delight with me as a toddler who has had a history of crying hysterically from "separation anxiety" leaps from his mother's arms to one of us at the nursery door. Carol, Judy, Carolyn, Dana, and I rejoice together when a child makes a breakthrough in spiritual understanding. Each one of these women is a different kind of flower who gives my life and my work a beautiful fragrance.

Others who complete my bouquet are special for many reasons. A glimpse of a few of these flowers appears in the book: Kathy, my sunflower; Angie, my pansy; Carol, my geranium, and Trish, my wildflower. When I think of Martha, I think of a lovely rose. Though I haven't known her long, she is a person in my life with whom I feel I can be totally open and honest, and whose honesty with me is valued and appreciated. Robin is a geranium to me. I look at the difficulties she is overcoming and admire her strength. As I arrange these blossoms in my mind, I find I have a bouquet of friendship that is already full and lovely. But, since a friendship bouquet is never complete, mine has room for many more flowers.

There is a wise adage that says, "To have a friend, you must show yourself friendly." Somewhere along the way, we must have shown ourselves friendly. There are many more friends of our heart that grow in our gardens—many that we talk and share with. Friendship is a gift from God. Because He is the Master Gardener, the friends He has planted in our lives will be our friends forever.

It [is] God . . . who made the garden grow in your hearts.

I CORINTHIANS 3:6 TLB

Friends Are Flowers in the Garden of the Heart

GINNY HOBSON

There are FLOWERS in my garden—
Friendships of the heart
That bloom with fragrant memories
Whether near or far apart.

The ROSE is the truest color,
The SUNFLOWER brings joy to my day,
The WILDFLOWER keeps me laughing,
And the LILAC shows me the best way.

Although we may want to change them,
It's true and everyone knows
Each FLOWER is unique and special,
And you can't make a wildflower a rose.

So in your garden of friendship
Cherish each FLOWER that's given;
For each one by design is a blessing
And a gift to you from heaven.

Clarence, the angel in the beloved film, *It's a Wonderful Life,* was right when he wrote, "No one is ever a failure if he has friends." Envision the friends in your life as you stand in your garden. Turn all around and see their faces and smiles. Friends are there when you need them to cheer you, uphold you, and share your life.

Someday soon, we hope you will find a moment to pen the memories of the friends blooming in the garden of your heart. Favorite flowers snipped and pressed into the pages of your heart are treasured keepsakes that will never fade away. When you journal these remembrances, those who follow after can learn what your friends meant to you during your lifetime. Sharing these stories expresses the best moments that life has to offer and inspires those dear to you to hold their own friendships close. Every heart has a story to tell. We encourage you to journal and share those special times. Memories are eternal.

Thank you for walking with us in the garden of friendship. May your own friendship bouquet be richly blessed, and may your life have the fragrance of the love you have given and received from friends.

Ginny Hobson & Sherry Morris

MY GARDEN OF FRIENDSHIP JOURNAL

For where your treasure is, there your heart will be also.

MATTHEW 6:21 NIV

The garden of the heart is beautiful place where the flowers of friendship bloom alongside a cascading fountain of shared experiences, thoughtfulness, and caring. Beneath an arbor of roses, our hearts find rest. Sitting near a lilac bush, we take in the fragrance and breathe more easily. The tulip springs up cheerfully in well-tended beds and decorates our view of our garden. Geraniums grow in pots along the path spilling resplendent blossoms into our lives. Tall and winsome sunflowers smile happily and spread the color of sunshine through our days joined in chorus by a laughing wildflower. Scented with memories, pressed flowers are treasures that we carry with us throughout our lives. Snipping and pressing favorite blooms into pages in our garden journal can become a keepsake that will never fade away.

Every garden has a place where plants are repotted, soil is nourished, and flowers are carefully collected and arranged into bouquets. A gardener takes special care of her treasures. We must also carefully tend the blooms that belong to us. Like flowers need rain and bees need pollen, the garden of friendship nourishes and sustains us from day to day through whatever life may bring.

Spend a little time giving thought to the friends who make your garden a colorful and splendid place. By journaling your thoughts, you may find your heart celebrating the garden of friendship for what it is— a treasure on earth that is a gift from heaven.

PANSY : CHARACTER TRAIT ~ YOUNG AT HEART

My friend who is like a PANSY to me: _____

Yesterday's a special memory until we meet again.
Time may pass, yet still we find we are the best of friends.

A memory of my friend: _____

_____

_____

_____

_____

_____

TULIP : CHARACTER TRAIT ~ SHARING

My friend who is like a TULIP to me: _____

Side by side or far apart, friends are always close at heart.

A memory of my friend: _____

_____

_____

_____

_____

_____

WILDFLOWER : CHARACTER TRAIT— JOY

My friend who is like a WILDFLOWER to me: _____

Time together is time well spent. Time with a friend is heaven sent.

A memory of my friend: _____

_____

_____

_____

_____

_____

LILAC : CHARACTER TRAIT— WISDOM

My friend who is like a LILAC to me: _____

A friend is someone who listens with her heart.

A memory of my friend: _____

_____

_____

_____

_____

_____

G E R A N I U M : CHARACTER TRAIT ~ ENDURANCE

My friend who is like a GERANIUM to me: _____

Love...hopes all things, endures all things. Love never fails.

I CORINTHIANS 13:7-8 NKJV

A memory of my friend: _____

_____

_____

_____

_____

_____

S U N F L O W E R : CHARACTER TRAIT ~ LOVE

My friend who is like a SUNFLOWER to me: _____

To love and to be loved is to feel the sun from both sides.

A memory of my friend: _____

_____

_____

_____

_____

_____

ROSE : CHARACTER TRAIT ~ FAITHFULNESS

My friend who is like a ROSE to me: _____

A true friend is a treasure of the heart.

A memory of my friend: _____

_____

_____

_____

_____

_____

PRESSED FLOWERS :

DEAR FRIENDS NOW GONE

My friend who is like a PRESSED FLOWER to me: _____

Time endures but cannot fade the memories that love has made.

A memory of my friend: _____

_____

_____

_____

_____

_____

Recipe for a Garden of Friendship Tea

Celebrate friendship by hosting *A Garden of Friendship Tea*. Tea and conversation create a wonderful atmosphere for celebrating the true gift of friendship. What do you need to host a garden tea? Inspiration for a garden tea theme is as endless as the variety of flowers that can grow in a garden. One idea is to make each guest feel special by presenting her with a gift that can be purchased or made inexpensively and placed at each table setting. A flower pin, a sachet of pot-pourri, a small friendship box, flower magnets, poems, bookmarks, and floral notecards are gift possibilities. If you are hosting a small and intimate tea, you might even choose to give each guest this book. A tribute to your friend could be written on the presentation page. Remember, the token of friendship you choose is not as important as letting your friend know that she is dear and special to you.

Helping people to connect and form relationships is important to all of us as we live in the next millennium. It is our hope that *Friends Are Flowers in the Garden of the Heart* will become a tool to encourage friendship in offices, church groups, and wherever else woman have the opportunity to form ties of caring. A friendship tea is good way to celebrate friendship, whether you use these suggestions or follow your own heart with other ideas.

LARGER TEA PARTIES

- Invite a guest speaker to talk about friendship.

- Consider using card tables to seat guests. Give them a conversation starter such as a sentence on a note card that reads, "My friend who is like a rose to me . . ." to encourage them to share. If you have several tables, assign each table a different flower to talk about and ask one speaker to share with the large group from each table.

- If your tea is for a church or office group, invite your guests to form "flower friends." Provide a small friendship box for every two people who would like to participate. Names may be drawn openly or secretly. Encourage "flower friends" to place small gifts or notes in the friendship box. Partners exchange the box back and forth between them for a definite period of time. Then, plan another friendship tea or gathering to reveal the secret "flower friend" or just to share how they were blessed and encouraged.

SMALL TEA PARTIES WITH CLOSE FRIENDS

BEFORE THE TEA:

- Hand address invitations to your guests, inviting them to a celebration of friendship.

- Remember, mixing friends at a tea is like having a beautiful bouquet of flowers on your table. Include on your guestlist friends from many circles. Your friends will be delighted, and new friendships may form!

- Choose table decorations. Include fresh or silk flowers.

- Select a friendship gift for each guest.

- Plan a simple menu. Cookies, finger sandwiches, fresh fruit, muffins or scones, or even just a great dessert are delightful tea fare.

- Choose a variety of teas and offer flavored sugar crystals or decorated cubes.

- Purchase or make a door prize.

DURING THE TEA:

- Celebrate friendship by reading a poem or anecdote from the book.

- Talk about the suggested care of friends.

- Read something from your friendship journal about each friend.

- Share a "personal moment" you have experienced with a rose friend or other flower of friendship. Invite your guests to share a special memory of a friend.

AT THE END OF TEA TIME:

- Talk about the importance of friendship in your lives.

- Give guests a note card and ask them to take time during the tea to write a note to a friend who has been special in their lives. Take up the cards at the end of the tea and mail them for your guests.

OTHER CONTRIBUTORS:
(IN ALPHABETICAL ORDER)

CARRIE BARNES (Tulsa, Oklahoma) is a ray of sunshine at Carpentree. A friend to both Ginny and Sherry, she is a sunflower to those who love her and have the joy and privilege of working with her.

VIRGINIA BRADFIELD (Sand Springs, Oklahoma) Ginny and Sherry's mom has many friends. All the tulips, lilacs, roses, and other flowers in her garden have taught the authors much about friendship.

JANE DEBORD (Temple, Texas) is a tulip friend to Ginny. Her story about her friendship with the Hobsons reminds us all of how some friends become family and bless more than one generation.

BECKY DODD (Tulsa, Oklahoma) also works for Carpentree. Like a butterfly who lights gently on a flower, her quiet spirit is a blessing in the garden of friendship to those who know her.

SUE RHODES DODD (Tulsa, Oklahoma) is a friend to Ginny and Sherry. Formerly Sue Rhodes Sesso, she is an editor for Honor Books and a cheerleader and mentor to the authors, who are grateful for this lilac.

LORENE HOPKINS (Sand Springs, Oklahoma) is a dear friend of Virginia's who has been there for her through thick and thin. She is also a lilac friend to Sherry and Ginny.

JENNIFER HOBSON LAMB (Tulsa, Oklahoma) is Ginny's daughter. Ginny and Jennifer have found the adage to be true: Having a daughter is like growing your own best friend.

CAROLYN MARBERGER (Tulsa, Oklahoma) came to work for Carpentree through her friend, Carole Palmer. They eat lunch together every day. Carolyn has risen above difficulties and is a friend to many.

MARTHA MEEKS (Sand Springs, Oklahoma) is Sherry's dear and special rose friend. Martha also contributed a story to Ginny and Sherry's previous book, *Seasons of the Heart.*

JULIA MOORE (Tulsa, Oklahoma) is the pen name of one who shared a personal story about her test of faith. Ginny and Sherry thank her for being willing to reveal her difficulties and how she learned from them.

CINDY PERRYMAN (Sand Springs, Oklahoma) is Ginny and Sherry's sister. On their family tree, Cindy is a branch that represents strength of character and resiliency. She is loved as both a sister and a friend.

DENISE ROUNDS (Tulsa, Oklahoma) is a friend of Ginny's in her Sunday school class. She writes about her sunflower friend in this book. Ginny thinks it takes one to know one.

DEE TABOR (Sand Springs, Oklahoma) shares an early lesson in friendship she learned from her mother's friend. A grandmother and a faithful member of her church, she is a flower loved by her many friends.

DIANE VILLINES (Tulsa, Oklahoma) is one of Virginia's many friends and a successful businesswoman. Her story about Virginia made Ginny and Sherry see their mom through the eyes of someone who is not family.

LAUREL YOUNG (Memphis, Tennessee) is a cousin to the authors. She is a true and dear rose friend to many, and as an only child, she has engrafted many of her friends into her family.

A friend is a present you give yourself.